SUFISM AND RELIGIOUS BROTHERHOODS IN SENEGAL

Sufism and Religious Brotherhoods in Senegal

by
Khadim Mbacké

Interpretive English translation by
Eric Ross

Edited by
John Hunwick

Markus Wiener Publishers
Princeton

Second printing, 2020

Originally published as *Soufisme et Confréries Religieuses au Sénégal (Etudes Islamiques*, no. 4), Dakar, 1995

For information contact to:
Markus Wiener Publishers
231 Nassau Sreet, Princeton, NJ 08542
www.markuswiener.com

Library of Congress Cataloging-in-Publication Data

Mbacke, Khadim
[Soufisme et confréries religieuses au Sénégal. English]
Sufism and religious brotherhoods in Senegal/ Khadim Mbacké; translated from the French by Eric Ross; edited by John Hunwick.
p.cm.
Includes bibliographical references.
ISBN 978-1-55876-342-5
1. Sufism—Senegal. 2. Islamic sects—Senegal.
I. Hunwick, John 0. II. Title.
BP188.8.S38M33 2005
297.4'8'09663—dc22

2004022892

Markus Wiener Publishers books are printed in the United States of America on acid-free paper, and meet the guidelines for permanence and durability of the Committee on Production Guidelines for Book Longevity of the Council on Library Resources.

CONTENTS

EDITOR'S PREFACE

I am pleased to be able to make available an English translation of Khadim Mbacké's very useful study of Islamic religious movements in Senegal. He put in my hands the task of editing it and getting it published when I visited him in the Institut Fondamental d'Afrique Noire (IFAN) at the Université Cheikh Anta Diop in Dakar in 1999. By then, his book *Soufisme et Confréries Religieuses au Sénégal*, had already been translated into English by Eric Ross—a researcher then in Senegal, and now a faculty member of Al-Akhawayn University in Morocco. His translation is "interpretive", i.e. not just literal, but inspired by his own knowledge of the topic, and made more easily readable in English, with a few added footnotes.

Among the items that I have added to the book are: a Glossary (p. v); some English language works in the Bibliography, with a second section to it on "Arabic Writings of Senegalese Sufi Authors", derived from Volume 4 of *Arabic Literature of Africa* in chapters on the Senegambian region, with which I was assisted by Ousmane Kane and Rüdiger Seesemann. My editing includes standardizing Arabic transliterations, with the format used in *Arabic Literature of Africa*, a few small changes of translated expressions; plus indexing, and computer formatting of the book to make it ready for publication. All numbered notes to texts are to be found in "Notes from Chapters", a section at the end of all chapters (p. 121), rather than as "footnotes"; as editor, I personally take responsibility for any 'technical' errors in the book

This book, in effect, reflects an aim of the Institute for the Study of Islamic Thought in Africa (ISITA), which I set up at Northwestern University in 2001. Now, with this book, you can all learn about the most major influence of Sufism in sub-Saharan Africa.

John Hunwick
July 2005

FOREWORD

The intent of this essay is to be an objective study of the state of Islam in Senegal and of the religious factors that influence it. It is hoped that it will permit those concerned by the question to reflect upon the future of Islam in that country in light of its past. Those who deal with the question of Islam in Black Africa must study each country individually in order to understand the Islamic concepts developed by a given society, concepts which are historically and culturally determined. This understanding in turn can help identify faulty concepts that are especially harmful to the religion itself, and that hinder the material and spiritual development of Muslims.

Islam in Senegal is characterized by the strong entrenchment of a certain number of Sufi brotherhoods. In effect, the majority of Senegal's 9,500,000 Muslims consider adherence to a brotherhood, a *ṭarīqa*, to be a religious obligation, in keeping with the well-known Sufi maxim "He who does not have a *shaykh* will have Satan for a guide." The largest brotherhoods in Senegal are the Qādiriyya (10.9% of the Muslim population), the Tijāniyya (51%), the Murīdiyya (30.1%) and the Layenne (6%).[1] Members of the largest brotherhood, the Tijāniyya, are distributed throughout Senegal while the second largest brotherhood, the Murīdiyya, is mostly concentrated in the historic provinces of Baol and Kayor, in the center of the country. As for the Qādiriyya, its membership is mostly concentrated in the Eastern provinces, though some Qādirīs may be found in other provinces as well.[1]

Islam's mystical brotherhoods were overtaken by Sufism, entering a phase of decline in the 6th century of the Muslim era (11th century CE). Sufism is a devotional practice which promotes the purification of the soul—a spiritual objective that lies at the very heart of Islam. The elimination of vices and strengthening of the soul through virtue is a fundamental Islamic precept, as God has said in the Qur'ān: "Truly he succeeds who purifies it. Truly he fails who corrupts it" (91:9-10). Such an important aspect of faith as purification of the soul, which impacts on happiness in this world and on prosperity in the next one, could not have been neglected by the Prophet "sent in mercy for creatures." How could he not have clarified this aspect of the Straight Path, he who brought religion to completion with the Qurʾānic revelation "This day have I perfected your religion for you" (5:3). Why is this perfected religion called "*al-Islām*", rather than "*al-taṣawwuf*" (Sufism)? Could those who invented the term "*taṣawwuf*" have given it content above and beyond the spiritual advancement and moral perfection of Islam? Does *taṣawwuf* represent the sublime essence and fullest observance of Islam, as its founders have claimed? If this is the case, is it not then incumbent upon us to judge the form of *taṣawwuf* practiced in a given country according to whether it has succeeded or failed to enhance that country's religious status?

The present study will first trace the genesis and evolution of Sufism in order to explain the circumstances that permitted the emergence of Sufi brotherhoods. Secondly, those brotherhoods which are currently active in Senegal will be briefly described as to the means and manner of their diffusion, the lives of their founding figures, their basic teachings, their internal organization, the links they maintain with each other, and the role they play in the country's cultural, economic, social and political life. An effort will also be made to discern in the present condition of Senegal's Sufi brotherhoods some indications of their future evolution.

The study will not, however, be simply an objective description of the situation. To the extent that the data permits, the Sufi brotherhoods will be subjected to critique. Only in this way can it contribute to a better understanding of Islam in Senegal.

Khadim Mbacké

GLOSSARY

A.H.	*Anno hegirae*- 'year of the *Hijra*, i.e. Islamic date, often compared with CE ('Common [Christian] era).
dā'ira	Association, organization.
dhikr	Lit. "mention", i.e. repeated mention of Allāh, and other divine names in congregational Sufi ceremonies led by a shaykh.
fiqh	Jurisprudence
ḥadīth	A saying of the Prophet Muḥammad.
ḥadīth qudsī	a saying of the Prophet with divine inspiration.
ḥajj / al-Ḥājj	*ḥajj* means 'pilgrimage' - to Mecca. *al-Ḥājj* - 'pilgrimist' is a title for a Muslim man who has performed the pilgrimage.
Hijra	The Prophet Muḥammad's 'migration' from Mecca to Medina (in 622 A.D.); and then the beginning of the Islamic calendar.
jihād	"struggle". generally battle against non-Muslims, seen as opponents.
kashf	'Unveiling' (i.e. investigation).
khalīfa	"Successor", i.e. title for a successor in leadership of a Sufi *ṭarīqa*.
muezzin	An English version of the Arabic word: *mu'adhdhin* -' caller to prayers'.
muqaddam	*Shaykh* of the Tijāniyya brotherhood, who is authorized to initiate new members.
(PBUH)	An abbreviation of "Peace be upon him", a rendering of the Arabic phrase *Ṣallā 'llāhu ʿalayhi wa-sallam* ("May God bless him and grant him peace"), uttered by Muslims whenever the Prophet Muḥammad is mentioned.
qāḍī	An executant of Islamic law.

Qur'ān	The sacred text of Islam; an Arabic term, often spelt in English as 'Koran'.
Ramaḍān	The ninth month of the calendar year of Islam, with daily fasting for Muslims from dawn to dusk.
shahāda	"Witnessing", is the first of the five canonical pillars of Islam and consists in testifying: "There is no god but God, and Muḥammad is the Messenger of God."
shaykh	"Leader" or "Senior man", a title applied to highly respected religious and learned men.
Sunna	The behavior and rulings of the Prophet Muḥammad.
Taalibé	French format from Arabic '*ṭālib*' = *Student, disciple.*
ᶜulamā'	"Scholars", especially of religious fields.
umma	the (world-wide) Muslim community.
waḥdat al-wujūd	"the oneness of being" or "the unity of existence"; a teaching of the early Sufi scholar Ibn al-ᶜArabī.
waẓīfa	A collection of prayers specific to the Tijāniyya. It is recited in mosques twice a day, mornings and evenings.
wird	Composition of pious recitations specific to each *ṭarīqa*.
zakāt	"Tax donation", the third "pillar" of Islam.
zāwiya	The home location for any branch of a Sufi *ṭarīqa*.

INTRODUCTION

The light of Islam began to shine forth onto humanity from the Arabian Peninsula in the 7th century of the Christian Era, when God Almighty chose Muḥammad (PBUH) as His messenger: "We have not sent thee but as a universal (Messenger) to men, yet most of mankind knows not ." (Qur'ān, 34:28) The Arab Prophet fulfilled his mission in its entirety and only departed this world, in 632 CE, after having educated a generation of believers capable of perpetuating the faith. Under the leadership of the first four caliphs, the "Rightly Guided" successors of the Prophet, his companions initiated great conquests in Asia, Africa and Europe. They communicated Islam to the most diverse peoples in these far-off areas.

Islam first reached Africa through the migration to Abyssinia of a group of some of the earliest converts to the religion. These were in essence refugees fleeing persecution at the hands of pagan Meccans. This event occurred before the migration of the Prophet to Medina and the beginning of the Muslim conquests. A generation later, Egypt and North Africa were among the first regions to be conquered. Somewhat later still, at a date which is difficult to determine precisely but can be approximated to the end of the 7th or beginning of the 8th century CE, Islam diffused southward, towards West Africa. This early contact of West Africans with Islam did not however signify their wholesale adoption of the new religion. Islam long remained the religion of a literate minority of Africans, a class of pioneers who propagated the Islamic message through peaceful means. Their proselytization eventually led to the conversion of chiefs and entire peoples.

Historians generally consider that this second stage in Islam's propagation in West Africa, with its initiation in Senegal, began in the 11th century CE, and have sought to link that to the activity of the Almoravids, who consequently are categorized as propagators of Islam. Though Islam was already present in West Africa, there is little doubt that the Almoravids did in fact play an important role in its diffusion there. More specifically, their greatest impacts

Africa around the 15th century CE, several centuries therefore after the introduction of Islam to West Africa.

At this point it is useful to look briefly at Sufism in order to define the term and to trace its evolution, an evolution which is reflected in its local Senegalese configuration. The consensus among Muslim historians and specialists is that the term *taṣawwuf* is etymologically derived from "*ṣūf*", or "wool", in reference to the coarse woolen garment worn by the ascetic precursors of the Sufis, or Muslim mystics. For them coarse wool was a sign of austerity, purity, and the renunciation of luxury. For al-Qushayrī, the 11th century CE Persian mystic, the term *ṣūfī* applied to groups of men united by their common commitment to *zuhd*–the renunciation of the superfluous things of this world–and their rejection of the slaughterous inter-divisions of Muslims, locked in fratricidal struggles over power. In their attempt to distinguish themselves from those they rejected, in the 2nd century of the Hijra (8th century CE) their successors adopted the name *ṣūfī*. Al-Junayd, one of the foremost Sufi masters of the 3rd century AH (9th century CE), defined *taṣawwuf* as follows:

> It is to render the heart independent of other creatures by purifying it, ridding oneself of natural instincts, extinguishing one's purely human qualities, avoiding the activities of one's natural instincts, and to acquire spiritual qualities, imbuing oneself with gnostic knowledge, giving preference to that which has eternal priority, giving good counsel to all members of the (Muslim) community, being entirely faithful to God and following the messenger in conformity with the *sharīʿa*.[2]

These ten constituent elements of the definition sum up the aims and objectives of Sufism, as well as the means by which one can cleanse oneself of vices and acquire virtues. Vices are primarily gluttony, idle talk, unrestrained search of fame, excessive love of material goods, exclusive attachment to life in this world, hate, jealousy, hypocrisy, and vanity. As for virtues, they consist of sincere repentance, fear of God, hope, renunciation of superfluous things, modesty, thanksgiving, faithfulness, patience, sincerity, truthfulness, love for, and trust in, God and the acceptance of His will. Sufis believe that by ridding himself of vices and acquiring virtues, a human becomes worthy of God's grace, and a friend so privileged that God loves him "becoming his sight through which he sees, his hearing through which he hears, and his hand by which he strikes", according to an oft-cited *ḥadīth qudsī*.

CHAPTER ONE

THE ORIGINS OF SUFISM

Muslim scholars who have studied the history of Sufism, and who have attempted to determine its origins, have come to discordant conclusions. Some have argued foreign influence in the form of an Aryan reaction; they maintain that Islam was imposed upon Persians and Hindus, but that it soon proved to be incompatible with their mentality. Islam in its pristine purity was not only rejected by them, but hey marked it with their own cultural forms in order to assimilate it. Other scholars have tried to establish a link between Sufism and Neoplatonism, the philosophical school that permeated Islamic culture beginning in the 2nd century of the *Hijra*. Yet others consider Sufism to be the result of Christian influence with specific links to Medieval Monism, with its capital notion of divine love. Others again believe that Sufism is the expression of a permanent and innate human tendency. Finally, there are those for whom Sufism's origin must be sought within Islam itself. Advocates of this internal explanation go so far as to claim that the Prophet Muḥammad laid the foundations of Sufism himself on the basis of divine revelation; the angel Gabriel is supposed, in this case, to have transmitted both *sharīᶜa* (explicit law) and *ḥaqīqa* (ultimate truth, source of Sufism). This latter part of the revelation was, however, only disclosed by the Prophet (PBUH) to those who were worthy of it.

Since the first manifestation of Sufism, in the southern Iraqi city of Basra, in the 2nd Muslim century, members of the *ᶜulamāʾ* have expressed divergent opinions as to the legitimacy of Sufis, and of the Sufi path. Some doctors of Islam considered Sufis to be heretics, and vehemently denounced and stigmatized their conduct. This is the case of Ibn al-Jawzī (d. 597 AH/1200-01 CE). In *Talbīs Iblīs* ("Satan's Quarrel"), Ibn al-Jawzī uses the following harsh words to describe Sufis:

> There is a group of pseudo-ascetics whose (spiritual) strength consists of being locked up in a mosque, a retreat, or a cave, while enjoying the public notoriety of their isolation (...) In order to justify

this practice, (the recluse) will sometimes claim he wants to avoid the detestable things he is likely to experience outside, whereas his (real) motives are pride and contempt for men. He fears losing the attention and the service he receives, and worries about maintaining his prestige and power. The company of men could constitute an unsettling factor for his prestige. He wants to be acknowledged and loudly praised. Sometimes his motives might be his attempt to hide his faults and defects, especially his ignorance. Thus does he enjoy being visited by all and sundry, while he himself will not visit others. Governors and hordes of plain people will troupe to his doorstep and kiss his hand, yet he will not visit the sick or accompany the dead to their graves.[3]

Other members of the *ᶜulamāʾ* consider Sufis to be the best of believers, engaged on the straightest of paths. This is the case of Al-Ghazālī (d. 1111) in *Al-Munqidh min al-Ḍalāl* ("Deliverance from Aberration") when he writes:

Sufis are those really engaged on God's path; their conduct is the best, their path the straightest, their moral standard the purest. Moreover, if all the rationalists, the philosophers and the agnostic thinkers, were to strive together to change the conduct (of the Sufis) for the better, they would not succeed.[4]

A third opinion among the *ᶜulamāʾ* represents a middle ground as exemplified by the great scholar Ibn Taymiyya (d.1328). According to him, there are three tendencies among Sufis: those Sufis who are committed to the very essence of Sufism; those Sufis who are content to bear the name only and for whom it is a source of livelihood; and thirdly those who subscribe to form alone:

...Men who strive the utmost in ritual practice... One can find among them people who, thanks to their efforts, succeed in reaching the highest rank and others who maintain an honest position among the People of the Right. In both groups one can find those who fail in their effort at interpretation (of the sacred texts) and others who transgress and who repent, or who do not repent. Finally, one can find among those who claim to be Sufis people who are unjust to themselves and who rebel against their Lord.[5]

Only the first tendency deserves the label "Sufi". Sufis of this sort are characterized by their observance of the obligatory religious practices, their avoidance of forbidden practices, their proprietary religious conduct, and their renunciation of superfluous, worldly, pursuits. Ibn Taymiya's attitude, which in our opinion is well founded, represents the position of moderate Muslim jurists. History has shown how a large number of Sufis have, in fact, deviated from the ideal due to the innovations introduced into Islam. Others have practiced Sufism strictly according to the rules of their discipline. To categorize them all as heretics is as unjust as to characterize them all as the best of believers.

> Then we have given the Book for inheritance to such of Our servants as We have chosen: but there are among them some who wrong their own souls; some who follow a middle course; and some who are, by God's leave, formost in good deeds; that is the highest Grace .(Qur'ān, 35;32)

This verse applies to Sufis, as much as to anyone else. Judgments in favor, or in condemnation, of Sufis may have been correct for certain periods of their history, or again for a minority among them. This can be demonstrated by studying the development of Sufism through three distinct phases. The first phase of Sufism was characterized by asceticism, the second by the *kashf* (or "unveiling") of gnosis, and the third by the theory of Unity of Being (*waḥdat al-wujūd*).

Renunciation (*zuhd*) of all that is superfluous is, as we have seen, the distinctive trait which characterized the early Sufis, hence their designation as *zuhhād* (ascetics) in the first and second centuries of the *Hijra*. In fact though, renunciation of futile and senseless worldly pursuits is a fundamental teaching of Islam, one reiterated time and again in the Qur'ān:

> Know, that the life of this world is play and amusement, pomp and mutual boasting and multiplying (in rivalry) among yourselves, riches and children. This is similitude. How rain, and the growth which it brings forth, delight (the hearts of) the tillers; soon it withers; you see it grow yellow; then it becomes dry and crumbles away. But in the Hereafter is severe punishment (for the devotees of wrong). And what is the life of this world, but goods and chattels of deception?" (57; 20), and "What is the life of this world but amusement an play? But verily, the home in the Hereafter, that is life indeed, if they but knew! (29;64).

Sufis, however, have a special understanding of renunciation of the world. The practices that result from this conception have varied between two extremes. Some Sufis deprived themselves completely of life's pleasures and mortified themselves in an effort to be free of carnal urges. These extreme ascetics would reduce their physiological and psychological needs in matters of food, sleep, and human company, to dangerous levels, in order to devote themselves entirely to day-time fasting and nocturnal prayer.

It appears that the practitioners of this form of asceticism are following the example of a specific group of Companions of the Prophet Muḥammad (PBUH). According to authentic *ḥadīth* reports, these companions asked the Messenger's wives about his supererogatory ritual practices. They must have misunderstood, or misinterpreted, the answers they received as one of them decided to observe a perpetual fast while a second decided on a lifetime of celibacy, and yet a third forsook sleep altogether. The Prophet, informed of the intentions of his companions, called an assembly of the Believers, and explained to them that excess was manifestly contrary to his Sunna (proper practice as exemplified by him). He further explained that Islam was simple in its rituals; there was neither need nor place for monism. Those who sought after extraordinary religious practices, practices beyond what he recommended, were not Muslims. This teaching of the Prophet was well understood by those ascetics properly versed in *ḥadīth* and its attendant legal precepts. They exercised the type of moderate renunciation essential to good Muslim practice. One of the most famous Muslim ascetics and jurists, Sufyān al-Thawrī, said:

> "Renunciation of the world consists in having humble ambitions, which is not the same as eating only pure food or waring course clothes. One can have possessions while renouncing the world just as one can be destitute and be attached to it. Leaving behind a sum of 10, 000 dinars, even if it means having to provide an explanation in the Hereafter, is preferable to me than having recourse to the charity of others. If material wealth was frowned upon in the past, today it shields believers from the need to solicit monarchs and the well-off.."[6a]

In effect, wealth has always been an excellent ally of the believer. We know that rich Companions, like ᶜUthmān b. ᶜAffān, provided decisive support to Islam in its hour of need. What is condemned is not wealth itself so much as the hoarding of wealth, the refusal to use it or invest it for the good of others. One must not become the prisoner of one's possessions, a "slave to the dirham and the dinar", in the words of the Prophet (PBUH).

Excessive renunciation was at one time quite common in Africa, where many thought that the perfect ascetic should have no house, as this would constitute a sign of attachment to mortal existence, while others neglected social obligations, because they were too absorbed in devotional practices.

The second period in the evolution of Sufism extended from the 4th to the 6th centuries of the *Hijra* (10th to 12th centuries CE). It was characterized by the concept of *kashf*, the "unveiling" of esoteric knowledge, and the diffusion of extremist ideas about "infusion in God" and "Union with God", all of which found support from a group of extremist Sufis inspired by al-Ḥallāj.

The concept of *kashf* was founded on the notion that God had created men so that they should adore Him: " I have only created Jinns and men, that they may serve Me ." (Qur'ān, 51:56). Yet men can only worship God if they know Him. Surely, innate knowledge can lead to faith, but the kind of knowledge that Sufis aspire to is of a higher essence than this. They derive it from a *ḥadīth qudsī*, which has had wide currency, but which is not acknowledged as sound by *ḥadīth* specialists, and which runs as follows: "I was a hidden treasure and I wanted to be known. Thus I created creatures that they might know Me." This kind of knowledge lies beyond the realm of discursive reason and can only be acquired through strong faith, continuous practice of mortification, and intense devotional exercises. It is a light, which springs from the purified heart of a being, and which "unveils" things, such as the nature of the divine attributes, the meaning of the divine names and acts, and the significance of eschatological symbols. Through the interpretation of inspired visions and dreams, this light can also reveal things about the remote past, or about future events. According to al-Ghazālī, the founding figure of this school of thought, this light guides men in the resolution of difficult religious questions, questions which otherwise would remain unanswered. This knowledge is thus more difficult to access and has wider applications than rational discursive knowledge. This can help explain why the study of the religious sciences in certain Sufi circles declined and why exaggerated and excessive practices took hold and eventually led these Sufis down paths which deviated from the Straight Path of Islam.

Some Sufis were clearly influenced by al-Ghazālī's admonition, in his *Iḥyā᾽ ᶜulūm al-dīn* ("The Revival of the Religious Sciences"), to "break all links and turn resolutely to God Most-High". They understood from this that only gnostic knowledge could constitute secure knowledge of God, and that they should pursue it exclusively. These Sufis seem to have forgotten that the acquisition of the religious sciences is essential to proper religious practice and its conformity to the Sunna, and that knowledge of these fundamentals constitutes the only sound basis for the spiritual promotion of Islam - the authentic expression of fear of God (or piety): "Fear God and He will instruct you", "And for those who fear God, He (ever) prepares a way out ." (Qur᾽ān 65:2). Advocates of *kashf* who nevertheless wanted to remain within the limits of Islamic orthodoxy warned their colleagues against considering this means as an end in itself. It could in this case lead to a form of idolatry, an insincerity of religious practice. Moreover, the Sufi who pursues *kashf* may be disappointed if, after long and intense practice, nothing is unveiled. This, in turn, could lead to an intensification and acceleration of dangerous devotional practices, causing at the very least marked antisocial behavior.

The life of al-Ghazālī, considered as a sure model by the founders and propagators of Muslim brotherhoods in Senegal, confirms this opinion. In effect, when al-Ghazālī embarked upon the gnostic path, he renounced his social responsibilities and isolated himself in mortification, reflection and meditation for ten years. He did however manage to write his greatest work, the *Iḥyā᾽ ᶜulūm al-dīn*, at this time.

The third period in the evolution of Sufism encompassed the 6th and 7th centuries of the Hijra (11th and 12th centuries CE). It was marked by the theory of Unity of Being (*waḥdat al-wujūd*) as proned by Muḥyī 'l-Dīn Ibn al-ᶜArabī (d. 638 AH/1240 CE).[6b] This theory can be defined as follows: Matter has no objective existence as its existence is dependent upon divine will. It is only our perception of matter which gives it a semblance of autonomous existence. Without human perception, perceived things would cease to exist, and only divine will would remain. Thus, the only real existence is that of God; all else is but appearance. In appearance, a single reality can be multiple and diverse, whereas in essence it retains its unity. *God is all, and all is God.*

For Sufis of this school, the ultimate object consists in annihilation (*fanāʾ*) of the being in God, the transcendence of apparent existence in favor of absolute, or essential, existence. As these ideas cannot be supported by Holy Writ, as it is understood by the majority of Muslims, advocates of *waḥdat al-wujūd* invented a three-tiered hierarchy of knowledge: discursive knowledge of truth, knowledge of the essence of truth, and direct contact with Truth (*al-Ḥaqq*). This gives the Qurʾān a double meaning, an exoteric discursive meaning, and an esoteric essential meaning. The first level of meaning corresponds to the first form of knowledge, while the second level of meaning is achieved through the second and third forms of knowledge. For example, knowledge of the existence of the Kaᶜba reflects the first form of knowledge, the vision of this sacred building reflects the second form of knowledge, while the third form of knowledge leads to an awareness of the hidden dimensions of the Kaᶜba's form and configuration as well as of the reasons men have been commanded by God to direct themselves to it in prayer. We have already encountered this form of knowledge in al-Ghazālī's conception of divine knowledge, the knowledge which allows men to know the Lord and draw closer to Him. Al-Ghazālī did not, however, aspire to annihilation in God (*fanā'*), as advocated by Ibn al-ᶜArabī. According to Ibn al-ᶜArabī, there are three levels to religion. The first consists of observing the five explicit ritual practices of Islam: declaration of faith, prayer, fasting, alms giving, and pilgrimage to Mecca, as most Muslims do. The second level of religion finds expression in personal, individual faith, in those who, like the *ᶜulamāʾ*, can grasp and demonstrate the foundations of faith. The third level of religion resides in gnostic knowledge of God and characterizes the Sufis, the "friends of God" (*awliyāʾ Allāh*).

Ibn al-ᶜArabī's doctrine is extremely dangerous to the extent that it implies that all humans: believers and unbelievers, good and bad, are right, and that reward, or punishment, in the Hereafter is unjustified, since the existence during which acts of obedience or disobedience were committed is not real; all appearance other than God is nothing but the appearance of a single reality—God. Ibn ᶜArabī was not only content to put forward these extravagant ideas but went as far as to proclaim himself the "Seal of the Saints", a pretension quite contrary to the Qurʾānic assertion that "saints" (*awliyāʾ*) are "friends" or "allies" of God who fear Him: "Behold! verily on the friends of God there is neither fear nor grief. Those who believe and (constantly) guard aganist evil." (10: 62-63). Likewise, the Sunna specifies that no period will be without saints until the end of days. The *ᶜulamāʾ* among Ibn al-ᶜArabī's contemporaries led a pitched battle against his deviations and demonstrated the incompatibility of the theory of *waḥdat al-wujūd*, with Islam as taught by Muḥammad (PBUH). The theory nonetheless spread throughout the Muslim world and influenced such important Sufis as Abū 'l-Ḥasan al-Shādhilī (d. 656 AH/1257 CE) and Ibrāhīm al-Dusūqī (d. 675 AH/1276 CE).

The brevity of this essay does not allow us to describe all the different tendencies which have marked the evolution of Sufism. Major works, such as *Qūt al-qulūb* by Abū Ṭālib al-Makkī (d. 696 AH/1296 CE), the *Risāla* of al-Qushayrī, al-Ghazālī's *Iḥyāʾ* and Ibn ᶜArabī's *Fuṣūṣ al-ḥikam* have dealt with these at length. The aim of this introduction to the subject consists of presenting the origins of Sufism so as to first highlight the theoretical foundations of the Sufi brotherhoods which have spread throughout the Muslim world, and then to present the sources of the thought and practices of a large number of Muslims, in Africa as elsewhere.

CHAPTER TWO

THE BIRTH OF SUFI BROTHERHOODS

Sufism is characterized by the great importance it places on the spiritual education of disciples. This is principally due to the fact that any given Sufi *ṭarīqa*, or "path"—and each path is considered by its members to be the best and most propitious one for attaining perfection in Islam—can only be transmitted through time and space by means of an educational system capable of producing Sufi masters. Sufi *shaykhs*, or "masters", have always been educators, disseminating spiritual education to their *murīds*, or "disciples". Originally however, these *shaykhs* did not aim at institutionalizing education into structured regimes or orders. Nor did they seek to unite their disciples in groups based on the teacher-student relationship. These developments characterized later generations of Sufis and ultimately led to the birth of Sufi brotherhoods.

In the 6th century AH (11th century CE) the Baghdad *shaykh* ᶜAbd al-Qādir al-Jīlānī (d. 561 AH/1166 CE) founded a *ribāṭ*, a hospice or meeting place, where he would meet with his *murīds* to inculcate his Sufi teachings in them. Fifty years later, after the death of their master and on the basis of his teachings, these disciples created an institution, the Qādiriyya *ṭarīqa*, with the aim of transmitting his teaching to future generations of Sufis. Since then, similar Sufi brotherhoods have sprung up under the direction of masters, or at the instigation of their disciples. In the 7th century AH/13th century CE alone several major *ṭarīqas* were created: the Badawiyya of Aḥmad al-Badawī (596-634 AH/1199-1236 CE), the Shādhiliyya of Abū 'l-Ḥasan al-Shādhilī (593-656 AH/1196-1258 CE), the Rifāᶜiyya of Aḥmad Rifāᶜī (d. 675 AH/1278 CE), and the *ṭarīqa* of Ibrāhīm Dusūqī (also d. 675 AH/1278 CE). These first brotherhoods, more or less founded on Ibn al-ᶜArabī's doctrines, produced among them over 37 different branches. Beyond this diversity however, the various *ṭarīqas* and their ramifications shared a number of fundamental ideas:

1. The path to God does not only lie in the observance of the prescribed ritual practices. Rather, aspirants along this path must fight an inner struggle to purify their souls, through mortification, abnegation and renunciation.
2. *Dhikr*, or "remembrance" of God through the cogitative repetition of his name and attributes, is the principal means of spiritual purification.
3. The *murīd* who aspires along this path must progress through a certain number of specified "stages" or "stations" (*maqāmāt*), namely, repentance, fear of God, hope, trust in God, satisfaction in God, etc. The *murīd* may also experience "states" (*aḥwāl*) of transcendence, special spiritual favors bestowed by God's grace that help the *murīd* along the aforementioned path.
4. The inner struggle to purify the soul can take many forms, some of which are appropriate to some individuals and not to others. Personal aptitudes and psychological profiles are therefore important to the process.
5. It is up to the *shaykh*, the Sufi master and educator, to determine which forms of inner struggle are appropriate to each disciple.
6. It is absolutely essential that aspirants along the Sufi path place themselves in the care of a *shaykh*.
7. Furthermore, the *murīd* must submit entirely to the authority of the *shaykh*, obey his orders and abstain from that which he proscribes. Yet the *murīd* must also love his *shaykh* just as unconditionally.
8. Among themselves, *murīd*s must instill a relationship based on solidarity and mutual aide (hence the term "brotherhood" applied to Sufi *ṭarīqa*s).
9. One cannot be a perfect Muslim without taking the Sufi path.

One of the most important principles shared by Sufi brotherhoods is their conception of the relationship between *shaykh* and *murīd*. A *shaykh* must be free of any desire to dominate, to have numerous disciples or to exercise power over people. He must find a time for meditation during which he frees himself from mundane preoccupations. He must know the individual situation of each of his *murīd*s; he must treat them with kindness, protect their rights, and refrain from exploiting their dependence on him.

He must not accept goods or services from his *murīds*, "except if, through divine inspiration, it is revealed to the *shaykh* that it is in the interest of the *murīd* that his gift, or offer of service, be accepted, because in this case the acceptance by the *shaykh* of the good or service is in the interest of the murīd and therefore will not jeopardize his integrity."[7] Finally, the *shaykh* must disapprove of any misconduct involving a *murīd*, but must do so in such a way as to maintain the transgressor's anonymity, not reveal confidential information, and give the reprimand an impersonal form.

As for the *murīd*, his obligations towards his *shaykh* are both more numerous and more ominous. The *murīd* must:

1. Renounce all will of his own and refer decisions to the will of his *shaykh*;
2. Keep silent in the presence of his *shaykh* and only speak when authorized to do so;
3. Abstain from casual behavior, such as raising of the voice, laughing out loud, chatting, etc.;
4. Be patient, not be in a hurry when visiting his *shaykh*, and wait for him, even if the wait is a long one;
5. Consider his position vis-à-vis his *shaykh*, like that of Moses in the company of Khiḍr (Qur'ān, 18: 61-83), meaning that he must follow his guide, even if the situation or behavior of the *shaykh* exceeds his understanding.
6. Not rest in the presence of the *shaykh* without his authorization to do so, but remain ready to serve him;
7. Not hide anything from his *shaykh*;
8. Not address the *shaykh* until he has ascertained his willingness to listen.

Many brotherhoods accept the possibility of a physical encounter with the Prophet Muḥammad (PBUH) after his death, and maintain that their founding *shaykhs* were accorded this privilege and received much of their mystic knowledge in this way. They rely here on a *ḥadīth* reported by al-Bukhārī, according to which the Prophet said "Whoever sees me in a dream will see me in an awakened state". This *ḥadīth* has been the object of six interpretations:

1. The *ḥadīth* is an analogy; whoever sees the Prophet in a dream *is like* the one who has seen him in reality. This is a reference to the fact that Satan cannot manifest himself in the image of the Prophet;
2. He who sees the Prophet in a dream will see the content of his dream come true;
3. The *ḥadīth* relates only to the Prophet's contemporaries, whoever saw him in a dream had the opportunity, thanks to God, to meet him in reality;
4. The dreamer saw the Prophet in the Prophet's mirror, so long as he was among those who were alive when this mirror existed (!);
5. The dreamer will see the Prophet in a special way on Judgment Day;
6. The dreamer will see the Prophet with his own eyes in his present lifetime.

It is this sixth interpretation which certain Sufis have used to substantiate the idea that their founding *shaykhs* saw the Prophet and were instructed directly by him. Al-Qurṭubī, the eminent jurist and Qurʾānic exegete, commenting on this sixth interpretation said "It is a proposition whose self-serving nature is self-evident. It would mean that the body of the Prophet leaves his tomb (in Medina) and that therefore we visit an empty tomb and address a void, since this so- called material vision can occur in daytime or at night anywhere in the world. Anyone with a modicum of intelligence would not even consider such a proposition."[8] We can offer a seventh interpretation: whoever sees the Prophet in a dream will see him in an awakened state *with the eyes of his mind*. If the Prophet were to speak to someone in a dream, the monologue might become imprinted in his mind and appear to him as if revealed in dictation.

In any case, recourse to an interpretation thatprecludes any notion of the Prophet (PBUH) returning to this world, is required for the following two reasons:

1.It is understood and acknowledged in Islam that the dead cannot come back to life, and that Muḥammad (PBUH) is truly dead as written in the Qurʾān "Truly thou wilt die (one day) and they (too) will die (one day) (39:30)", and "And Muḥammad is no more than a messenger; messengers have already passed before him; and if he dies or is killed, will you turn back upon your heels?" (3:144).[9] Moreover, there is no sound *ḥadīth* to support the possibility of a return of the Prophet (PBUH) to life in this world.

2.Only a quarter of a century after the Prophet's death his own Companions went to war, one against another, and his very grandson, Ḥusayn b. ᶜAlī b. Abī Ṭālib, was assassinated. These terrible events caused permanent fractures within the *umma*. Yet, despite the gravity of this situation, the Prophet did not reappear to put an end to the dissension. Were it possible for him to return to this world, is it conceivable that he would have missed the opportunity of doing so during the terrible *fitnas*, at a time when his guidance could have set the Muslim community back on the course of harmony and unity?

For these reasons we can reject the 4th and 6th interpretations cited above. We believe that the dreams of Believers constitute one of the forty parts of prophecy, and that God can bestow knowledge through dreams upon whomever He pleases. He can inspire whomever He wants with whatever He wants. However, to be considered as authentic, all knowledge or inspiration received in this manner must conform to the *sharīᶜa*, the accepted and acknowledged corpus of law. It is clear, moreover, that knowledge acquired through divine inspiration cannot supersede knowledge imparted by divine revelation.

Notwithstanding their numerous doctrinal similarities, Sufi brotherhoods have vastly different policies on administrative, or organizational, issues. They may diverge in the manner of pledging fidelity to the *shaykh*, or on secondary aspects of the *shaykh-murīd* relationship, or again on the content of *dhikr* and the manner of its practice. In these matters, each Sufi brotherhood is likely to be influenced by the social and cultural environments in which it becomes established. Generally speaking, in urban areas brotherhoods tend to be moderate, concerned with education and proper religious observances, and open in their relations with non-members, whereas, in rural areas, brotherhoods are often characterized by strict adherence to internal regulations, intransigence, strong bonds among members, inordinate reverence for *shaykhs* and fanatical devotion to them. Countless brotherhoods have disappeared into oblivion after ignorant *shaykhs* took control of them, leading them astray into all sorts of heresies, far from their original forms. Other *ṭarīqas* have survived as institutions. Their relative strengths and weaknesses will vary, depending on the cultural level of the people who adhere to them, and on the relations they have with temporal power. Generally speaking, brotherhoods do well today in environments where ignorance reigns and are weak in those with a high level of Islamic culture. Moreover, brotherhoods that have close relations with the state will enjoy its support, whereas those that are hostile, or even indifferent, to it, are likely to be repressed in one way or another. This helps us to understand why Sufi brotherhoods are so popular in Africa today and relatively weak elsewhere. Their popularity on the African continent has much to do with their assimilation of traditional African customs and elements, such as transmission of spiritual power through genealogy, the excessive importance accorded to a person's birth, the equation of spiritual guides with traditional chiefs, extended polygamy, etc.

We can now turn our attention to the situation of the various Sufi brotherhoods that have spread through Senegal in the past century and a half. We will discuss them in chronological order: the Qādiriyya *ṭarīqa*, the Tijāniyya *ṭarīqa*, the Murīdiyya *ṭarīqa*, and the Layèene.

CHAPTER THREE

THE QĀDIRIYYA *ṬARĪQA*

The Qādirī *ṭarīqa* is named for *Shaykh* ᶜAbd al-Qādir al-Jīlānī (470-561 AH./1077-1166 CE.). This Sufi *shaykh* was born in Naïf, a village in the Iranian province of Jilan, on the south shore of the Caspian Sea. It is there that he learnt the Qurʾān and was introduced to the fundamentals of the Islamic sciences. At age eighteen he went to Baghdad, where he studied Arabic under al-Tabrīzī, *ḥadīth* under a number of masters, including Abū Saᶜīd al-Makhzūmī, and Ḥanbalī and Shāfiᶜī *fiqh* (jurisprudence). ᶜAbd al-Qādir was then initiated into Sufism under *Shaykh* Abū 'l-Khayr Muḥammad b. Muslim al-Dabbās (d. 1131 CE.). His Sufi master set up a school in Baghdad which ᶜAbd al-Qādir was given the task of running. He taught there for a while before opening his own *ribāṭ* (spiritual center) around 1133 CE. where people would assemble on Friday mornings, Sundays and Mondays to hear his sermons.

His sermons were often about the need for total renunciation of worldly pursuits on the part of those newly embarking upon the Sufi path, though once they had progressed somewhat along this path they might return to them. Many were so impressed by what he had to say, by his commitment to renunciation, his humility, and the manner in which he enjoined good and refrained from baleful acts, that they become more or less permanently attached to him. It is said that he exhorted people, even the destitute, to give liberally to the *shaykhs*. Presents flooded into the *ribāṭ* from various provinces of the Caliphate. These were used to feed the needy who flocked to hear his sermons. *Shaykh* ᶜAbd al-Qādir performed *ḥajj* (pilgrimage to Mecca) sometime between 1095 and 1127, was married in 1114 and is reputed to have had 49 children. He died in Baghdad in 1166 CE. and was buried there.

He left a number of written works, the most famous of which are *al-Ghunya*, a treatise on law and Sufism, and *Futūḥ al-ghayb* ("Revelations of the Unseen"), where he puts forth his views on Sufism as first expressed in his sermons. According to this latter work, ᶜAbd al-Qādir's conception of the relationship between the educator *shaykh* and the *murīd* follows the description already provided above. His views are also similar to those of his contemporary Abū Ḥafs ᶜUmar al-Suhrawardī (1144-1234 CE.), a Sufi and a statesman, author of a work entitled *ᶜAwārif al-Maᶜārif* ("The Growth of Gnosis").

Here follow some of ᶜAbd al-Qādir's thoughts, chosen for what they reveal about the content and nature of the type of Sufism which still bears his name. He is reported to have told his disciples: "Follow and do not deviate; obey unconditionally; practice perfect patience and do not demonstrate opposition; wait without losing hope; practice *dhikr* together; purify yourselves of sin, and remain attached to your Lord."[10] As to the conduct proper to the believer, he said:

> "Do not complain to others about the fate that is your lot by (God's) will; on the contrary, demonstrate thankfulness and joy. Do not commit yourself entirely to any human being; reveal your inner self to no-one (...) If you feel love or hate towards someone, scrutinize his acts in light of the Qur'ān and the *Sunna*. If these acts are good and proper, then love them, if not you must detest them. (This) will prevent you from loving or hating arbitrarily. God Most High says: "Nor follow the lust (of your heart), for it will lead you astray from the Path of God. Surely for those who go astray from the Path of God is a grievous punishment, for they forget the Day of Reckoning" (38;26). Abandon someone only to (please) God; this means: abandon him only if you see him commit a major transgression, or if he persists in a venial sin."[11]

Many miracles have been attributed to *Shaykh* ᶜAbd al-Qādir al-Jīlānī and have been greatly embellished by his disciples. The *shaykh* himself does not seem to have accorded any importance to such phenomena. He said:

> "I saw a great light which filled the horizon and an image rushed towards me calling: "ᶜAbd al-Qādir ! I am your Lord, and I make licit for you all prohibited (things)." "Silence! O damned one" I replied. And the light became dark, and the image turned to smoke. Then a voice said "ᶜAbd al-Qādir! You have resisted by your persistent observance of your Lord's commands and your discernment of the states inherent to spiritual practices. I have been able to lead astray seventy men from among those on the Sufi path". "Thanks to God" I said. When ᶜAbd al-Qādir was asked how he knew that he was dealing with Satan, he replied "Because of his claim, I make licit for you all prohibited (things)".[12]

These are but some of the teachings *Shaykh* ᶜAbd al-Qādir wanted to inculcate to his *murīds* to serve as basic rules for their communal activities.

The *ṭarīqa* that institutionalized this project was only really established in the early 11th century CE, some fifty years after the death of the *shaykh*, by descendants who succeeded to his spiritual legacy: *Shaykh* ᶜAbd al-Wahhāb (1157-1196 CE), *Shaykh* ᶜAbd al-Razzāq (1134-1206 CE), and *Shaykh* ᶜAbd al-Salām b. ᶜAbd al-Wahhāb (d. 1214 CE).[12] It is through the activities of these *shaykhs* and other disciples that the Qādiriyya *ṭarīqa* spread from Baghdad to other parts of the Muslim world, first throughout the Middle East and Egypt, to the point where, by the beginning of the 19th century CE., nearly every Muslim country had branches of the Qādiriyya brotherhood. However, for the most part, these various Qādirī *ribāṭs* were, and remain, independent of each other. Despite the regular visits they organize to ᶜAbd al-Qādir's tomb in the original "mother" *ribāt* in Baghdad, their relations with the central spiritual authority of the *ṭarīqa*, such as it is, are weak.

The Qādiriyya probably reached the Moroccan city of Fez through the activities of two of *Shaykh* ᶜAbd al-Qādir's descendants: Ibrāhīm (d. 1196 CE in Iraq) and ᶜAbd al-ᶜAzīz, who settled in Andalusia and the descendants of whom fled to Morocco shortly before the fall of Granada in 1492. It is even possible that this *ṭarīqa* reached North Africa prior to this, as cultural and commercial ties between the Maghreb and Egypt, where the Qādiriyya found an early base, were very strong, and because of the pilgrim traffic to and from Mecca, where the *ṭarīqa* was present as of the 13th century CE. In any case, initially the early

Qādirī community in the Maghreb did not actively involve itself in trying to propagate the brotherhood locally or exporting it southwards towards West Africa.

It is the *ribāṭ* (known in the Muslim West as a *zāwiya*) of Marrakech which eventually undertook this kind of activity and served as base for the diffusion of the brotherhood to Timbuktu (through the Kunta *zāwiya*) and Mauritania. Some historians have argued that the Qādiriyya *ṭarīqa* reached the Niger Bend as of the 15th century CE. in the person of Muḥammad b. ᶜAbd al-Karīm al-Maghīlī (*c.*1498). What is sure is that the Kunta *zāwiya* and its various off-shoots played the key role in propagating the brotherhood in the Western Sudan. A Senegalese researcher has argued that the Qādiriyya only reached Senegal in the 19th century.[13] What he may be referring to here is the propagation of the brotherhood throughout the country. Given the long attested presence of Moors in the Senegal River valley and areas further south, and given also the frequency and intensity of cultural and commercial exchanges in this area, it seems unlikely that the Qādiriyya was not present before the 19th century. For centuries the acquisition and perfection of Islamic learning had led Senegalese Muslims to study in Mauritania, while the pursuit of material and alimentary security had led Moors ever deeper into Senegal. These types of mutually beneficial relationships could be most easily secured within a brotherhood type structure of spiritual alliance. Moreover, the Idaw 'l-Ḥājj were established on both banks of the Senegal River by the 17th century and had established solid cultural and genealogical links with the sovereigns and inhabitants of the kingdom of Waalo. They then settled throughout that country and even into the neighboring kingdom of Kayor, where they established villages like Waadaan, Ndogal, etc., before becoming totally assimilated into the local population. The Idaw 'l-Ḥājj are the ancestors of the present Darmanko.

Generalized diffusion of the Qādiriyya *ṭarīqa* in Senegal did not in fact occur until the end of the 18th and beginning of the 19th centuries. The phenomenon was the result of the activities of the families and affiliates of al-Mukhtār al-Kuntī (d. 1811) and of *Shaykh* Muḥammad al-Fāḍil (d. 1869). *Shaykh* Sīdiyya al-Kabīr

(1780-1868) and *Shaykh* Muḥammad al-Fāḍil in particular had wide renown throughout Western Sudan as spiritual masters and they served as Sufi guides to many Senegalese disciples. They are the ones responsible for the establishment of the Qādiriyya in their respective areas of activity. Members of *Shaykh* Sīdiyya's family, as well as those of *Shaykh* Muḥammad al-Fāḍil, most notably his son *Shaykh* Saᶜd Būh, criss-crossed the Senegalese countryside organizing their respective followings and in each town of any importance they designated a representative to oversee relations between the local *shaykhs* and *murīds*, making sure that the collection of the *hadiyya* (or "donations" in money, or in kind, destined for the *shaykh*) was properly conducted. Members of these families settled permanently in these regions.

This is how Kayor and Soninke provinces like Galam and its neighbors became Qādiriyya territories. The Qādiriyya *ṭarīqa* did not however achieve the same results in Futa Toro. It was nonetheless the principal *ṭarīqa* of Senegal during the whole of the first half of the 19th century. Thereafter it underwent a marked decline, due for the most part to the campaigns of the great Tijānī *Shaykh*, *al-ḥājj* ᶜUmar Tall (d. 1864), who led people to abandon the Qādiriyya and to follow him both spiritually and physically.[14] The ᶜUmarian attempt to stem the growth of the Qādiriyya in favor of the expansion of the Tijāniyya led the Qādiriyya *shaykhs* to intensify their own efforts in order to secure their position and the influence they exerted over their disciples. In effect, by this time Senegal's Muslim population was so attached to the Sufi brotherhoods that it no longer distinguished between its Muslim identity and its Sufi affiliation, and affiliation to a given brotherhood was itself increasingly becoming an inherited trait, rather than a matter of personal choice.

It is said that the Qādirī *Shaykh* Saᶜd Būh b. Muḥammad al-Fāḍil dispensed the Tijānī *wird* to all those who wanted it. He was seeking in this way to transcend the sectarian divisions between *ṭarīqas* and to demonstrate the equal validity of each of them. His policy can be attributed to two factors: first, his status as a *sharīf*—a descendent of the Prophet Muḥammad (PBUH)—may have led him to adopt a flexible attitude towards the brotherhoods, serving all Muslims without distinction. Secondly, a very material consideration cannot be overlooked: *sharīfs* receive donations from their followers. Naturally, the more followers a *sharīf* has, the greater the quantity of donations he will receive. Service to all without distinction made good business sense. Donations made during *Shaykh* Saᶜd Būh's visit to Senegal in February and March 1913 have been calculated at 70,000 francs. He is reported leaving Louga and Saint-Louis with forty camels loaded with merchandise destined for his Mauritanian encampments.[15]

In this same period, a nephew of *Shaykh* Saᶜd Būh, *Shaykh* Maḥfūẓ (1855-1919), settled in the southernmost part of the country, in the Casamance. After numerous and extensive travels through Senegal and Guinea, where he met up with Samori Toure and Mūsā Molo, both of whom showered him with gifts, he founded the village of Dār al-Salām in 1902. In his biography of his father, *Shaykh* Maḥfūẓ's son *Shaykh* Shams al-Dīn tells us that, at the beginning of his ministry in Casamance, the local Diola population was openly hostile to *Shaykh* Maḥfūẓ. He was only able to make significant headway after establishing a collaborative relationship with the French colonial authorities. According to *Shaykh* Shams al-Dīn:

> When our *shaykh* and father first arrived, they (the Diola) thought he was European. They had never seen a (white) Muslim preacher before. Some of his disciples warned him against trying to settle in Diola country. When he asked them about this, they cited as evidence the great number of pigs among the Diola, their lack of hygiene, and mostly their unbelief. He replied that there was nothing bad in all of this, and that despite it, if God wills, he would guide the Diola to Islam. Once he was firmly established among them, the pagans came to him to submit to Islam, but the *shaykh* for his part also went to visit their chiefs. Each of them would slaughter one to ten, or sometimes as many as twenty, cows to feast him. To this must be added the many gifts and the white coins of that day. He would call them to Islam to save them from paganism and ignorance, (and exhorted them) to do good and acquire noble qualities.[16]

Shaykh Maḥfūẓ assembled his disciples in his other village of Binako and put them to work. They grew millet, rice and groundnuts in the fields around the village. They were also active in other economic sectors appropriate to their environment, including the exploitation of natural resources. In exchange for these services, the disciples were taught the Qur'ān and some elementary principles of Islam.

It is important to note here that it is *Shaykh* Saᶜd Būh who commanded *Shaykh* Maḥfūẓ to go and settle in Senegal. He did so following one of his tours of the country, when he returned to Mauritania with a considerable quantity of goods unobtainable there. There is no risk in overemphasizing the role played by the search for material necessities in inciting Mauritanian *shaykhs* to undertake proselytization trips to Senegal; the sources clearly indicate that the search for the necessities of life was the economic context behind their decision to settle permanently there.

Despite the competition it now has to endure from local *shaykhs*, the family of *Shaykh* Maḥfūẓ continues his mission in Casamance. Even for *Shaykh* Shams al-Dīn, who founded Dar al-Khayr in 1937, the emergence of local *shaykhs* was worrisome. This *shaykh* complains in his writings of the jealousy of some of his black neighbors, who would dispute his status as *sharīf*, and the attendant right to be revered, to receive *hadiyya* (offerings), and *ziyāra* (pious visits). He was further worried by the fact that these same *shaykhs* were claiming these privileges for themselves and were organizing *gamous* (local pilgrimages) to mark the *mawlid* (the Prophet Muḥammad's birthday), events which would draw large crowds. According to *Shaykh* Shams al-Dīn, the best way to celebrate the *mawlid* is to honor the descendants of the Prophet (PBUH) by visiting them and offering them numerous presents, because they are the biological representatives of the Messenger of God. Moreover, it seems as though *Shaykh* Maḥfūẓ would also give the Tijānī *wird* to all those who requested it, just as his paternal uncle *Shaykh* Saᶜd Būh did - and for the same reasons. This behavior was severely critiqued by Tijānī *shaykhs*, some of whom refused to recognize the validity of any initiation to the Tijānī *wird* bestowed by a *shaykh* who also used the *wird* of another *ṭarīqa*. This position is in keeping with the teachings of *Shaykh* Aḥmad al-Tijānī, and will be discussed below.

The problem of *wird* was also the object of much debate among the *shaykhs* of Futa Toro when relations between the Qādiriyya and the Tijāniyya soured in the late nineteenth and early twentieth centuries. In *al-Ḥaqq al-mubīn fī ukhuwwat jamī*[c] *al-mu'minīn* ("The Plain Truth about the Brotherhood of All Believers"), *Shaykh* Mūsā Kamara (1864-1945) explains that "the fanaticism and ignorance of the adherents of the Tijānī *ṭarīqa* lead them to proclaim the incompatibility of their *wird* with any other." The author cites as an example of this the case of the disciples of *Shaykh* Sa[c]d Būh who while attending a session of Tijānī *dhikr*, wanted to join in. The Tijānīs objected under the pretext that, as the Qādirīs had not received the *wird* from a Tijānī *shaykh*, they could not recite it together. This Tijānī exclusiveness, according to *Shaykh* Mūsā Kamara, was the product of vulgar men who mistook themselves for Sufi masters. By this time the TijānīsF of Futa Toro were so divided amongst themselves that they would no longer pray with each other.

In any case, the decline in influence of the Qādiriyya *ṭarīqa* in Senegal continued throughout the latter half of the 19th century. In Futa Toro the decline progressed to the point where the Qādiriyya was nearly entirely eclipsed by the rise of the Tijāniyya. This was in part due to the vigor of *al-ḥājj* [c]Umar Tall's movement, but also because the Qādiriyya did not possess a strong local center able to sustain its fortunes in this province.

In other parts of the country, in the Wolof areas for example, the situation improved. Qādirī *shaykhs* settled in Jolof, while in Kayor *Shaykh* Muḥammad al-Kuntī, better known as Bū Kunta, founded the village of Ndiassane, 5 km. South of Tivaouane. Initially at least, this *shaykh* was more involved in economic and business activities than in religious ones. In *Etudes sur l'Islam au Sénégal*, Paul Marty maintains that *Shaykh* Bū Kunta never had a *wird,* but that he was surrounded by a group of religious scholars who transmitted the Qādirī *wird* under his authority to those who sought it. Whatever the case may be, he was able to attract adherents in Senegal's large cities. His own chosen representatives oversaw religious activities in these communities. According to Marty, *Shaykh* Bū Kunta's adherents numbered 50,000, most of whom were originally from Mali. This branch of the Qādiriyya is independent of *Shaykh* Muḥammad Fāḍil's *zāwīya*, which is represented in Senegal by the family of South of Mauritania. When in Senegal, he is hosted at the Qādirī *khayma*, a residence in one of Dakar's working class neighborhoods. The *khayma* ("pavilion") is where the capital's Qādirīs assemble for *dhikr* on Friday afternoons, especially if there is a visiting Mauritanian *shaykh* in town, or for special religious ceremonies. Senegal's Qādirīs remain divided between these two founts of authority. *Shaykh* Bū Kunta's branch has the advantage of being a home-grown Senegalese organization, while *Shaykh* Saᶜd Būh's network operates by means of Mauritanian *shaykhs*, representatives, and organizations.

It is the Mauritanian *zāwiya* which has launched new initiatives in recent years which aim at reviving the Qādiriyya in Senegal, giving it popular appeal and new life in the face of the country's other brotherhoods. These activities are centered on the city of Thiès, considered a Qādirī bastion. A federation of local Qādirī associations was created in April 1988 under the high auspices of *Shaykh* Ḥaḍramī [Adramé] Ould Sīdī Buya and of *al-ḥājj* Muḥammad Lamine Kane, Honorary President of the High Council of Qādirīs of Senegal. The federation elected Mr. Doudou Niang as President (20 April, 1988).[17] The very unfortunate events of 1989 between Senegal and Mauritania had a detrimental effect on the *ṭarīqa*. Some long-established Mauritanian *shaykhs* were killed, while others had to go into hiding for months to escape from the rage of excited mobs. Their cousins in Mauritania waited for years before the border between the two countries was reopened and once again allowed to be crossed. Things are progressively returning to normal and one now sees Mauritanian *shaykhs* presiding beside Senegalese religious figures, just as in the old days.

CHAPTER FOUR

THE TIJĀNIYYA *ṬARĪQA*

The Tijāniyya *ṭarīqa* [the Tijāniyya] emerged in the Maghrib during the last decades of the 18th century. It was founded by *Shaykh* Aḥmad b. Muḥammad b. al-Mukhtār b. Sālim al-Tijānī, born in 1727 in ᶜAyn Māḍī (Algeria). According to his biographers, he had memorized the Qurᵓān by the age of seven. He next studied the basic texts of the Mālikī school of jurisprudence: Ibn Abī Zayd's *Risāla*, the *Mukhtaṣar* of Khalīl, and the *Muqaddima* of Ibn Rushd. It is only then that he embarked on the Sufi path. At sixteen he took over the administration of the *zāwiya* founded by his grandfather, where he taught the Qurᵓān. He then studied for a number of years in Fez, under the *ᶜulamāᵓ* of that city famed for its Islamic learning. When he returned to teach in his home town he attracted a large number of students.

In 1762, at the age of thirty-six, *Shaykh* Aḥmad al-Tijānī performed *ḥajj* to Mecca. It was during this trip that he visited Sufi centers in Cairo and Tunisia and became successively affiliated with the Qādiriyya, the Nāṣiriyya and the Khalwatiyya *ṭarīqas*. He returned to Fez and began teaching the Sufi ideas which would later serve as doctrinal foundation for the Tijānī *ṭarīqa*. The *ṭarīqa* was established after the *shaykh* had secluded himself in deep devotion and intense meditation which culminated in a vision in which "he saw the Prophet (PBUH). The Prophet ordered him to leave the *ṭarīqas* he had joined and bestowed on him the function of *khalīfa* of the Messenger."[18] In 1781, in the village of Samghoun, "he was ordered by the Messenger (PBUH), in an awakened state, and not in a dream, to educate all men without distinction, and he was given the *wird* he was to transmit."[19] He returned once more to ᶜAyn Māḍī where he worked to establish the *ṭarīqa* and spread its teachings among Muslims. This enabled him to travel through many parts of North Africa, where he acquired disciples, opened *zāwiyas*, and instated *muqaddams*.

Shaykh Aḥmad al-Tijānī's reputation grew, and his *ṭarīqa* became large enough to worry the Turkish government, which still ruled Algeria. Government forces besieged ᶜAyn Māḍī. As usual, or rather as is God's will, material force, however large, could not stop the diffusion of ideas and beliefs. In matters such as these, the use of military force, rather than hindering the diffusion of a proscribed idea, can actually help to diffuse it, sometimes far beyond what the advocates of the banned idea could have accomplished on their own. Life became more difficult for the *shaykh* following this incident. There was dissension among his disciples in ᶜAyn Māḍī which he was unable to resolve. He left Algeria for Morocco where he obtained the support of the Sultan, Mūlāy Sulaymān. He opened a *zāwiya* in Fez and resumed his educational activities. The city of Fez then became the main center for the diffusion of the Tijānī *ṭarīqa.*

The *shaykh* dictated his fundamental doctrines to two of his disciples: Sīdī ᶜAlī Ḥarāzim and Muḥammad al-Mushrī al-Sayhī. The former consigned what had been dictated to him by the master in a work entitled *Jawāhir al-Maᶜānī fī fayḍ Sayyid Abī 'l-ᶜAbbās Aḥmad al-Tijānī* ("The Pearls of Meaning from our Master..."). This book is considered sacred by the brotherhood.

When the *shaykh* felt that his end was approaching, he set out to resolve an important problem often neglected by other founding *shaykhs*: that of the spiritual succession of the master. In fact, many brotherhoods have been ripped apart by internal strife over this question. *Shaykh* Aḥmad al-Tijānī designated his disciple, the *muqaddam al-ḥājj* ᶜAlī b. *al-ḥājj* ᶜĪsā Tamasīn, as his *khalīfa,* with the added stipulation that the caliphate of the *ṭarīqa* would thereafter alternate between his own descendants and those of Tamasīn.[20] The question having been resolved, *Shaykh* Aḥmad al-Tijani was called back to his Lord on 19 September 1815.

Doctrines of the Tijānī Tarīqa

The Tijānī *ṭarīqa* was distinguished from the outset by the belief of its founder that its founding principles and doctrines were dictated to him *in a wakened state and not in a dream* by the infallible Messenger, the Prophet Muḥammad (PBUH). By implication, this belief entails the infallibility of the doctrines themselves; any teaching transmitted by the Prophet can neither be erroneous nor questionable. We are justified therefore in scrutinizing closely the contents of this message. According to *Shaykh* Aḥmad al-Tijānī, the Messenger set forth the principles of the *ṭarīqa* in these terms: "Keep on this path, without withdrawing into seclusion, and without putting an end to interactions with other men, until you reach the station which is your due."[21] This *ṭarīqa* is supposed to be easily put into practice, as it does away with the privations and mortification which characterized previous brotherhoods. It also entails social functions, as there is perceived to be a need to work in the field, to identify ills and find remedies for them.

The remedies usually consist in the recitation of the *wird* and *dhikr*. The practice of *dhikr* is not obligatory for Tijānīs. If they opt for the practice, it must be done mornings and evenings. The practice of *dhikr* does not however dispense one from reciting the *wird*. Whoever omits the *wird* must immediately make up for it. This is not the case for those who do not practice the *waẓīfa*. The *waẓīfa* is a collection of prayers specific to the Tijāniyya. It is recited in mosques twice a day, mornings and evenings. The *dhikr* of Friday afternoons is called the *haylala* and is obligatory. Like the *waẓīfa*, the *haylala* should be recited collectively, in groups.

The Tijānī *wird* is as follows:

- "I beg forgiveness of God" 100 times,
- the *Prayer for the Prophet* 100 times,
- the *shahāda* 100 times.[22]

To this main Tijānī *wird* are added a number of lesser ones, known as "*zāwiya wirds*", or as "common *wirds*". This may include: reciting the request for forgiveness 100 times (whatever the actual wording), reciting the *Prayer of* the *Opening* (*Ṣalāt al-Fātiḥ*) 100 or 50 times, reciting "*Allāhu Aḥad*" ("God is One") 200 times, and reciting al-Tijānī's *Jewel of Perfection* (*Jawharat al-Kamāl*) 12 times.[23]

Shaykh Aḥmad al-Tijānī promised the love of the Prophet (PBUH), access to saintly status, and many similar favors to all those who practiced his *wird*. "Whoever acquires the well known *wird*, inherent to the *ṭarīqa*, from me, or is initiated by someone authorized by me, will go to Paradise, as will his parents, his wives, and his descendants, both indirect and non-direct (*sic.*), so long as he does not insult others or show hatred or enmity to others, and so long as he maintains love for the *shaykh* and practices the *wird* until the end."[24] In theory, the Tijānī *wird* can only be acquired through an acknowledged master. Such masters are rare today, if we take into consideration the qualifications specified in the *Jawāhir*. According to this work, such a master is especially hard to find, as he is likely to be pursuing the path anonymously, concealing himself and perhaps even acting in a vulgar or ignorant fashion. In this case these acts will not be held against him. In fact they are not even real, as the one who seems to be committing them has been annihilated in God. In practice, one goes to a Tijānī *muqaddam* to be initiated into the *ṭarīqa* and receive the *wird*.[25]

The use of Tijānī *wird* and *dhikr* is subject to a number of conditions, the principal one being a proper affiliation to the Tijānī *ṭarīqa*. The need for proper affiliation is often reiterated in *al-ḥājj* ᶜUmar Tall's *Kitāb al-rimāh* ("Lances"). According to it, the *shaykh* who transmits the Tijānī *dhikr* must :

1. Be authorized to initiate (new members) by the supreme authority of the *ṭarīqa*, or by some other properly constituted authority;

2. Not be in possession of another *wird* received from a non-Tijānī *shaykh*;

3. Not visit any living *wālī* ("saint") or the tomb of one;

4. Regularly, and publicly, perform the five obligatory daily prayers and respect all other religious prescriptions;

5. Remain faithful and sincere in his love for the *shaykh* (Aḥmad al-Tijānī) until his death and consider (the *shaykh*'s) successors equally;

6. Not believe himself to be immune to God's tricks;

7. Never insult others, or show any hatred or enmity towards others on account of his faithfulness towards the *shaykh*;

8. Recite the *wird* until his death;

9. Have strong faith;

10. Refrain from criticizing and from attracting criticism;

11. Be authorized to practice *dhikr* after a suitable initiation;

12. Attend the *wazīfa* and *dhikr* sessions on Friday afternoons;

13. Only recite the *Jawharat al-Kamāl* (Jewel of Perfection) when in a state of ritual cleanliness obtained through ablution with water;

14. Not create trouble between people, and especially between brothers;

15. Not postpone *dhikr* without good reason;

16. Not initiate new members without the proper authorization;

17. Respect all brothers;

18. Maintain corporal cleanliness and wear clean clothes whenever possible;

19. Face the *qibla* (the direction of Mecca) in a seated position;

20. Speak only when necessary;

21. Represent in his mind the figure of the model (the Prophet Muḥammad) from the beginning until the end of the *dhikr* session;

22. Meditate the meaning of the words in the *dhikr* if he is able to understand them.[26]

Given the importance that Tijānīs place on the recitation of Aḥmad al-Tijānī's *Prayer of* the *Opening* and *Jewel of Perfection*, we are providing the full texts in translation here:

Ṣalāt al-Fātiḥ (Prayer of the Opening)

> O God, bless our lord Muḥammad who opened what was sealed, who closed what came before, who caused Truth to triumph through Truth; bless his family, according to its merit and the immense respect due it.[27]

The *Prayer of the Opening* is worth 6,000 recitations of the Qur'ān, according to *Shaykh* Aḥmad al-Tijānī. How could it be otherwise since it was produced for him by *an angel on a platter of light*? "When I had finished it" said the *shaykh*, "I realized that the devotion of men, jinns, and angels, weighed less that it did."[28]

Jawharat al-Kamāl (Jewel of Perfection)

O God, bestow Your grace and salvation from the source of divine mercy, brilliant as a diamond, true in the truth that surrounds the center of intellects and thoughts, at the light of being which has formed man, to him who possesses divine truth, to the great bolt of lightning which pierces the clouds, precursors of the beneficial rains of divine mercy, and illuminates the hearts of those whose knowledge is as deep as the ocean and who seek union with God, at the bright light which fills Your being and encompasses all places.

O God, bestow Your grace and salvation from the source of truth which penetrates the tabernacles of realities, from the source of knowledge of the straightest, the most complete, the only true path.

O God, bestow Your grace and salvation from knowledge of truth through truth, at the most sublime of treasures, all liberality comes from You and returns to You, in the sphere of colorless light.

May God bestow His grace on him and his family, grace through which, O God, You will reveal him to us.[29]

Al-ḥājj ᶜUmar Tall and the Expansion of the Tijānī ṭarīqa in Senegal

The Tijānī *ṭarīqa* spread through North Africa during the lifetime of its founder and was next established in Mecca by North African pilgrims. It is precisely in that holy city that a young West African pilgrim by the name of ᶜUmar b. Saᶜīd Tall met a Tijānī *muqaddam* named *Shaykh* Muḥammad al-Ghālī, one of Aḥmad al-Tijānī's companions, and was initiated, or rather was confirmed, into the Tijānī *wird*. On his return to Senegal, *al-ḥājj* ᶜUmar Tall would propagate the *ṭarīqa* there and in adjoining countries.

Al-ḥājj ᶜUmar Tall was born in 1796 in the village of Halwar, Futa Toro (modern Department of Podor, Senegal). He had memorized the Qur'ān by the age of thirteen, and then went on to study Arabic language and grammar, Islamic law, and the rules of Qu'ānic recitation, first in his native Futa Toro, and then in the famous school of Pire, in Kayor. He was first initiated to Sufism by *Shaykh* Mawlūd Fall al-Shinqīṭī and *Shaykh* ᶜAbd al-Karīm al-Nāqil of Futa Jallon, who taught him the Tijānī *wird.* In 1827 he performed *ḥajj* to Mecca, where he met *Shaykh* Muḥammad al-Ghālī. He would later say of him:

> I submitted entirely to him, remained in his service for three years, which confirmed my initiation. He taught me the necessary *dhikrs*, established me within the *ṭarīqa*'s chain of transmission and never ceased promoting my spiritual progress through new *dhikrs*. Thanks to him I was enlightened in complete conformity with formal and substantial law."[30]

The most important result of *al-ḥājj* ᶜUmar Tall's internship with *Shaykh* Muḥammad al-Ghālī was that his master designated him as *khalīfa*, or supreme representative, of the Tijānī *ṭarīqa* in Black Africa. According to ᶜUmar Tall, "the *khilāfa* ("caliphate") signifies the lieutenancy of the *shaykh* (Aḥmad al-Tijani), whom the *khalīfa* replaces. In effect, the *khalīfa* gives disciples what the master would have given them: *dhikr*, *wird*, hidden meanings, directives, objectives to be attained, spiritual retreats, rules of conduct to be observed, gnostic science and knowledge. In short, he operates on them, and in them, as the master would have. Therefore he has the same rights as the master because, given his status, he stands in lieu of him.[31]

If *Shaykh* Aḥmad al-Tijānī was the confirmed *khalīfa* of the Prophet, then *Shaykh* ᶜUmar Tall was for his part the confirmed *khalīfa* of the *khalīfa* of the Messenger of God. Because he was responsible for implementing the teachings of an infallible authority, he enjoyed something of infallible status himself. In the *Rimāḥ*, *al-ḥājj* ᶜUmar Tall provides us with numerous arguments confirming the legitimacy of his caliphate. He relies heavily on dreams. He cites one of his companions who saw the Messenger (PBUH) in a dream. The Messenger said "*Shaykh* ᶜUmar must call all of God's servants to God's religion, and must give them all necessary explanations. I am his guarantor; he should not worry about the people of Futa; they have little faiths."[32]

After his pilgrimage, *al-Ḥājj* ᶜUmar Tall set out at a very leisurely pace towards home, visiting all the major Islamic states along the way. He went first to the Bornu Sultanate, where he resided until he came into conflict with its sultan. An attempt on his life forced him to flee Bornu for the Sokoto Caliphate, where he remained for seven years at the court of Muḥammad Bello, son of *Shaykh* ᶜUthmān Dan Fodio. After marrying one of Muḥammad Bello's daughters, he left Sokoto for the Dina of Masina, where he was for a while warmly received by the Emir, *Shaykh* Aḥmad Lobbo. He next headed for the Emirate of Futa Jallon, where he lived for six years. It is only in 1842, after an absence of fifteen years, that he returned to his native Futa Toro, only to leave again the following year to embark upon his political and military career.

In effect, as soon as he returned to his homeland, *al-Ḥājj* ᶜUmar Tall decided to unite Muslims under his authority in order to lead them against the pagans who lived among them. He began by mobilizing his compatriots, and then asked Muslims in adjoining countries to join him. To justify his military project, he declared that "battle against infidels is the task to which I have committed myself - until the power of Islam replaces that of unbelief... As *ᶜulamāʾ*, it is we who have the responsibility of propagating the religion of God, of restoring the prestige of Islam in Futa Jallon, Segou, Nioro and Karta, because unbelief is rampant there. Once this battle is won, it will be easy to combat the Christians. Surely the Islam in which we believe does not countenance compromise with infidels. Whoever revels in their company is one of them."[33]

Shaykh ᶜUmar had given serious thought to the state of religion in West Africa and had reached the conclusion that recourse to arms would be necessary if an Islamic state was to be established in the region. However, for a number of reasons listed below, he failed in his political and military project:

1. He did not raise the awareness of Muslims in Futa Toro and its adjacent regions sufficiently to lead them to fully understand and support his initiatives;

2. He acted as *khalīfa* of the Tijāniyya *ṭarīqa* and sought to obtain the adherence of his followers to that brotherhood despite the fact that most Muslims in the area were already members of the Qādiriyya *ṭarīqa*;

3. His movement, at least initially, was an ethnically based Toorodo, or Tokolor, movement;

4. He waged war against Muslims in Masina, an acknowledged Islamic state, and this fratricidal act alienated the sympathies of many who might otherwise have joined him;

5. Last but not least, he was faced with the strong opposition of a colonial power intent on imposing its domination over all of Senegal and West Africa and on crushing any nationalist movement in its way. In order to thwart his project, the colonial power, already staunchly anti-Islamic, did not hesitate to exploit the factors listed above.

However, though *al-Ḥājj* ᶜUmar Tall failed to unite West Africa Muslims in a single Islamic state of Tijānī inspiration, he was successful in spreading the Tijānī *ṭarīqa* in all the countries in which he was militarily involved. Moreover, he designated preachers and teachers who carried on this task through peaceful means in other areas as well: first in Futa Toro, then in other parts of Senegal.

It has been argued that the growth of the Tijāniyya at the expense of the Qādiriyya in Futa Toro was due to the "democratic" nature of the former and the spirit of equality that characterized it. Yet, adherence to the Tijāniyya did not bring about any notable change in the attitudes or behavior of the inhabitants there. Slavery continued to exist, and even free men were subdivided into a dozen different castes: nobles, warriors, men of religion, fishermen, smiths, praise singers, etc. Even today, Tokolor society maintains these hierarchies and distinctions between people, to the extent that inter-caste marriages are proscribed, and all this with the approval of its religious elite.

In any case, the Tijāniyya took firm root in Futa Toro before spreading elsewhere in Senegal. This phenomenon was entirely due to *al-Ḥājj* ᶜUmar Tall, to his disciples, and to the disciples of his disciples. Some of this expansion was peaceful and some of it took the form of warfare.

When *al-Ḥājj* ᶜUmar Tall disappeared from the scene in 1864, in Bandiagara at the eastern extremity of his campaigns, his war was resumed in the west by another Tijānī *Shaykh*, Muḥammad Ba, better known as Maba Diakhou. Maba Diakhou's project resembled that of his predecessor; he aimed at uniting Muslims within a single Islamic state powerful enough to repel infidels from the *Dār al-Islām*. He expressed as much in his letter to Pinet Laprade, the French Governor of Saint Louis:

> To Laprade, Commander of the Christians,
>
> Reflect carefully upon what I say. Listen to me and do not lend an ear to the claims of infidels, hypocrites, and villains. Between us there is only a commercial treaty. As for the inhabitants of Jolof, I only fought them because they had fought, killed and imprisoned Muslims. I sent three emissaries to the Burba of Jolof to ask him not to attack Muslims, but he refused. That is why I fought him.
>
> Know now that Jolof, Sine and Baol do not belong to you. Since you insist on claiming the contrary, explain to me why you do nothing to stop unbelievers from oppressing Muslims (in these countries).
>
> O Laprade, I am neither unjust nor jealous. Anyone who commits an injustice towards Muslims will have God as judge between himself and me. No, no, Laprade! Be a brother to me, as I will be unto you; no agreement I commit to will be broken by me.
>
> According to God's religion, infidels are unjust. And God perfects His light despite infidels, and despite those who associate (something else with Him). Surely God does not amend the acts of corrupters. Do not violate an oath once given.[34]

Maba Diakhou focused his diplomatic and military efforts on those countries mentioned in his letter to the Governor. His home base was in Salum. He initiated a mass migration of Muslims from neighboring states to Salum in the hope of turning it into the core of the new Islamic *umma* he was attempting to build. Famous scholars and deposed kings alike were attracted to his side and came to lend support to his mission. The ambitious Imam of Salum was able to raise a large Muslim army with which he waged war against pagan forces, defeating them several times before being defeated himself by an alliance of pagan and colonial forces at the battle of Somb in 1867.

Though he was a Tijānī himself, Maba Diakhou, unlike *al-Ḥājj* ᶜUmar Tall, does not seem to have emphasized this aspect of his mission and certainly made no attempt to pressure his allies and associates into joining the *ṭarīqa*. He was mostly interested in the eternal and universal aspects of Islam, and this helps explain why Qādirī *shaykhs* joined his forces and supported his cause. He did not therefore play an important part in the spread of the *ṭarīqa*, and this holds as well for the Tijānī warriors who joined him in Salum.

The most important agents in the expansion of the Tijāniyya *ṭarīqa* in the post-ᶜUmarian period were the educator *shaykhs* who were not connected to the warfare endemic at the time. These educators were too numerous for us to be able to survey all of their contributions here. We can only cite as examples *al-Ḥājj* ᶜAbd Allāh Niasse and his children, who did much to spread the *ṭarīqa* in Salum, in the Gambia, and further east in Ghana and Nigeria for instance. Based in Kaolack, they are still very active in the fields of Quʾānic teaching and the Islamic Sciences. Other Tijānī masters who were active in Senegal include: *Shaykh* Mu'ādh Ka and his family, *Shaykh* Aḥmad Deme of Sokone, *Shaykh* ᶜAbd Allāh Cissé of Diamal, *Shaykh* Muḥammad Bamba Sall and his family (they had been Qādirīs, but *Shaykh* ᶜUmar converted them to the Tijāniyya), the disciples of *Shaykh* Aḥmad (defeated and killed inthe battle of Samba Sadio, 1875) who are represented today by the family of Amary Ndack Seck of Thiénaba.[35] *Shaykh* Mālik Sall of Louga, *Shaykh* Saᶜīd Ba of Médina-Gounasse, etc. However, of all the Tijānī teachers in Senegal, the most active was *Shaykh* Mālik b. ᶜUthmān, better known as *al-ḥājj* Mālik Sy.

The Diffusion of the Tijānī ṭarīqa by al-ḥājj Mālik Sy

Mālik Sy was born in Gaya, a village to the North-East of Dagana, in Waalo, in 1855. He learnt the Qur'ān as a child, and then proceeded to study Arabic and the fundamental Islamic sciences: *tawḥīd* (theology), *tafsīr* (Quranic exegesis), *fiqh* (jurisprudence), etc. He was initiated to the Tijānī *wird* by his maternal uncle, Alpha Mayoro Welle, who himself had received it first from *Shaykh* Mawlūd Fall and then from *al-ḥājj* ʿUmar Tall. Mālik Sy performed the *ḥajj* to Mecca in 1889. On his return, he established himself first in Saint Louis, the colonial capital of Senegal, then in the nearby Gandiol region, and then in 1895 in the village of Ndiardé near Pire, where he both taught, and worked the land. Many young students were attracted to his rural establishment; he would teach them the Qur'ān and the basic principles of the Islamic sciences, in return they would cultivate his fields for him. He remained in Ndiardé until 1902. In that year he set out to visit Saint Louis and Louga, and then established himself permanently in the town of Tivaouane. In Tivaouane he opened a *zāwīya*, and dedicated himself entirely to teaching, but he nonetheless continued to administer rural estates in Ndiardé and Diacksao.

Al-Ḥājj Mālik Sy's pedagogy was classical in both content and method. Students would begin by memorizing the entire Qur'ān. By approximately age eighteen, students would complete this phase and most would leave the *zāwiya* to rejoin their families. They would pursue agricultural or commercial activities, or they might open up Quranic schools of their own where they could transmit some of what they had acquired. Some bright students however remained in the Tivaouane *zāwiya* with *al-Ḥājj* Mālik Sy in order to continue studying. They would then be introduced to works such as Ibn Mālik's *Alfiyya*, the *Mulḥat al-iʿrāb* of al-Ḥarīrī, and the *al-Ājurrūmiyya* in grammar, the *Risāla*, and the *Mukhtaṣar* of Khalīl in law, al-Akhḍarī's *Sullam* in logic, and the *Muʿallaqāt*, a collection of classical Arab poetry.[36] Students were taught in groups of six to ten under the supervision of a professor. Professors were specialized in various fields and were closely connected to *al-Ḥājj* Mālik Sy, who did much of the teaching himself. Students came from all over Senegal and would vary in number from about 80 to 250. There were no fees for studying at the *zāwiya*, but parents would usually send many gifts in kind to *al-ḥājj* Mālik Sy, and students would work in their master's fields during the agricultural season.[37]

Al-ḥājj Mālik Sy resided in Tivaouane until his death in 1922. While a resident of the town, he had made several trips to Dakar, the great new colonial capital, and had established a Tijānī *zāwiya* there. This *zāwiya* remains to this day an important cultural center and it has played a major role in the diffusion of the *ṭarīqa* and the continued renown of its founder. Likewise, *al-ḥājj* Mālik Sy's trips to other urban centers lead him to acquire many new disciples and to designate *muqaddams* to represent him. This was especially the case in Saint Louis, Dakar and Rufisque, which constituted, along with Gorée, the "Four Communes": the political, economic, and cultural nerve centers of the colony.

On reading *al-ḥājj* Mālik Sy's works it becomes apparent that this *shaykh* was more intent on spreading Islamic culture in Senegal than in propagating the Tijānī *ṭarīqa* per se. He had in fact come to the realization that, although Senegalese society clearly identified itself as an Islamic one, it remained ignorant of some the most basic principles of the religion, hence his emphasis on education. He saw it as his mission to provide the knowledge without which religious practice becomes meaningless. Certainly he would transmit the Tijānī *wird* to those worthy disciples who requested it, but he did not impose it on anyone. Nor did he try to get people to abandon the Qādirī *ṭarīqa* for the Tijāniyya. He was careful lest he be seen favoring this kind of sectarian conversion.

Nonetheless, like other Tijānī *shaykhs*, *al-Ḥājj* Mālik Sy was convinced of the superiority of his *ṭarīqa* over all others, and of the claim of its founder to be the "Seal of the Saints". He deployed considerable talent and energy in praising *Shaykh* Aḥmad al-Tijānī and his ideas. The apologetic works in favor of the *ṭarīqa* dominated the religious literature of that time. This was due on the one hand to the fact that the *ṭarīqa* was systematically attacked by scholars and ignoramuses alike, and on the other to the difficulty of producing a scientific discourse that could convince the open-minded.

What is undeniable is that *al-Ḥājj* Mālik Sy possessed the highest degree of Islamic culture, that he lead an exemplary life, and that he had earned the highest esteem of his contemporaries among the *ᶜulamāᵓ* . The positions he took relative to the important questions of the day, and the nature of his relations with the colonial authorities are proof of his uncommon intellect and insight. While reasoning according to religious criteria, he arrived at the conclusion that he could only succeed in his mission if there were peace and tranquillity, and he would need to establish a regular working relationship with the political regime. Consequently, he adopted the appropriate attitude towards it. This explains his decision to settle permanently in the town of Tivaouane and his desire to see his colleague and Tijānī brother, *Shaykh* ᶜAbd Allāh Niasse, settle in Kaolack. This was a deliberate demonstration to the French authorities that there was nothing to hide and that they had nothing to fear from the Tijāniyya.

We can gain a cursory impression of *al-ḥājj* Mālik Sy's religious ideas from a 220 page work of his entitled *Kifāyat al-rāghibīn*. This is less a work of erudition than a summary of the vast corpus of books the author had read. Due to the apprehensions of the colonial authorities, few books on Islamic subjects were printed in Senegal at the time, and fewer yet from abroad were allowed into the colony. Yet despite this, and because of his good relations with the regime, Mālik Sy was able to obtain the most important contemporary works from the Muslim heartland. In *Kifāyat al-rāghibīn*, the author cites many scholars as authorities and then offers his own short comments, leaving no doubt as to his opinion on the topics being discussed. His opinions are not necessarily supported by citations from the Qurᵓān or the *Sunna*. In fact, *al-ḥājj* Mālik Sy was not a specialist in *ḥadīth*; he cites *ḥadīth* uncritically, without recourse to the usual caution and verification. Instances of this include the following: "My companions are like stars; you can find the right direction by following one or another among them", and the famous "Differences between imams are a source of divine mercy",[38] both of which are categorized as weak or even doubly apocryphal in the authoritative texts on *Sunna*.

The author's comments, scattered throughout the work, are particularly revealing in that they show his rejection of a number of reprehensible habits and practices of contemporary Senegalese society.[38] Among these we can cite: the practice of taking more than four wives at a time, the practice of putting one's hand on the forehead of a *shaykh* to express reverence, taking excessive pride in one's birth, selling amulets, imams and muezzins accepting salaries, women reciting *dhikr* out loud, the use of religion for personal monetary gain, embezzlement of *zakāt*. With regard to this last point, the author is indignant:

> Look at how some of our compatriots are in the habit of giving their *zakāh* (obligatory alms) to the landlord as rent-money, or to a *shaykh*, or to their elder brother, even though the verse (9: 60, which defines use of alms) can only be applied to them if they fulfill the conditions specified and justifying the transfer. You can even see some who transfer *zakāt* from one locality to another, so distant that a traveler from one to another is allowed to shorten his prayers, despite the fact that non-transfer is a well known condition for validation.

Elsewhere, in response to Sufis who claim the privilege of acting in ways that contradict formal religion, the author maintains that if esoteric or substantial laws contradict the exoteric ones, they are invalidated. No authentic inspiration can contradict the Qur'ān or the *Sunna*, and divine revelation (*waḥy*) ceased with the closing of the prophecy of God's Messenger.[39] How then could this *shaykh* not ask himself how the *Ṣalāt al-Fātiḥ* came to be transmitted to al-Tijānī by an angel? After all, ideas such as those put forth in works like *Jawāhir al-Maʿānī* have encouraged Sufis to adopt precisely the kinds of attitudes that *al-Ḥājj* Mālik Sy is stigmatizing.

Another revealing comment in the *Kifāyat al-rāghibīn* tells us something of the author's religious thought:

> A *shaykh* must direct the attention of his disciple to the necessity of venerating all authentic *shaykhs* and of respecting all Muslims, and to the fact that despising someone else's *ṭarīqa* is equivalent to despising Islam. This could lead the disciple into infidelity, as he would begin to speak ill of others, to be jealous, and this would divide believers. We implore God to protect us from conceit.[40]

At the end of the book the author provides an anecdote which can be seen as summing up his religious philosophy:

> The minister 'Abū Ṣāhib, who was Christian, came to visit the *qāḍī* Ismāᶜīl. The *qāḍī* rose to greet him, but observed the disapproval of the other guests present. When the minister had left, Ismā'īl told them "I understand your disapproval, but God Most-High has said: "God does not forbid you (from doing good) to those who have not fought you because of religion..." This man ('Abū Sahīb) satisfies the needs of Muslims and is an intermediary between us and Al-Muᶜtaḍid (the Caliph). My gesture (of greeting) was charitable." And the guests were quiet.[41]

The attitude of the *qāḍī* falls far short of that which *al-Ḥājj* Mālik Sy recommended to his son, Aboubakar Sy, and which the latter had published in the Moroccan newspaper *Al-Saᶜāda* on 16 September 1913 (that is, shortly after that country had come under French "protection"), as follows:

> Praise be to God, whose reign is the only eternal one, whose power is the only eternal one. Prayers and blessings on the best of prophets, the Prophet of cities and the Prophet of deserts, on his family and companions, people of merit and right.
>
> From the creature most in need of the mercy of his Master, *al-ḥājj* Mālik, son of the *shaykh*, the jurist, the generous ᶜUthmān, may our clement Master bestow on both the oceans of His kindness and His satisfaction.
>
> To all who adhere to the Tijānī *ṭarīqa*, and to other Muslims, who want the peace of Islam, and who live in Senegal: Salvation, mercy and benediction of God Most-High, whose grace and kindness never ceases to envelop us.
>
> I recommend that you strengthen your faith and your confidence in God Almighty, and that you remain strongly united.
>
> Adhere completely to the French Government. God (may He be blessed and exalted), by His grace, has granted special victory to the French. He has chosen them to protect our persons and our possessions. We must therefore live in perfect harmony with them, that they may not hear anything about us that might lead to suspicion.

Before they came, we lived as captives, with murder and pillage. Muslims and infidels were equal in this regard. Had they not come, we would still be in that state, and maybe worse...

He who looks on the French with an enlightened mind, who considers how God has granted them victory and peace, will not contravene their orders.

Brothers, do not succumb to the words of idiots who will tell you that the end of French power is at hand. These are pernicious shadows. Firm knowledge of God demonstrates the opposite.

Do not consider it a bad thing to have to pay the taxes they have instituted. For a clear mind it is obvious that this is a contribution they request of you, not a burden they have imposed.

On the contrary, be wary of the heavy duties some would like to see you pay under the designation "pious offerings". Has our *shaykh* and intercessor, Aḥmad b. Muḥammad al-Tijānī (may God Most-High be pleased with him), not prohibited these offerings, except when they are given with pleasure.

God Most-High has said: "Do not eat your goods unjustly between you". The wages for management of souls are God's alone. God (Sublime and Exalted is He) revealed many times to Muḥammad (PBUH): " Tell them - I ask no wage of you..."

Trust the French as they trust you. Is not the reward for kindness, kindness itself? Do not be led astray by the appearance of texts. Cling firmly to divine wisdom; your hearts will rejoice in peace. Time, for he who uses it, is blessed. Otherwise it is harmful. Know that the French have given full support to our religion and to our country. You would understand this if you were intelligent.

If I had more time I would provide you with proof of this from Qur'ānic verses and prophetic traditions, but what I have said is sufficient. Good bye!

Written on Tuesday 14 Ramaḍān 1330 of the Hijra. Blessings and salvation on the Immigrant Saint.

Greetings on the part of the author of these lines, Babakar Sy, son of *al-Ḥājj* Mālik Sy, by order of his father.[42]

The attitude expressed in this letter was not shared by all Senegalese *ᶜulamā*ʾ . Many were those who would not keep silent when they saw that the infidels, the colonizers, were in fact fighting them because of their religion, by blocking the teaching of Arabic through various means, for instance.

Numerous regulations to this effect were in fact enacted. Two examples will suffice to demonstrate this. The first one is a decision of Governor Faidherbe dated 22 June 1857. He forced all those who wanted to open a Qurʾānic school in Saint Louis to solicit permission from the colonial administration. Authorization would only be given if the one asking for it fulfilled the following three conditions:

•be a resident of Saint Louis, or have lived there for seven years;

•prove before an examination board that he had sufficient knowledge;

•obtain a certificate of good morals and behavior from the mayor of the city.

The second case is a regulation, dated 9 May 1896, which stipulates that it was illegal to open a Quranic school without the authorization of the Government General. Prior to obtaining this authorization, one had to get a notice from the municipal authorities and a go-ahead from the Director of the Interior. The candidate had to present his case before the aforementioned Director and produce a clean criminal record and a certificate of good morals and behavior from the municipality where he intended to open his school. Another condition for obtaining authorization was that the candidate had to submit to an admissibility test in front of a commission composed of the mayor, the *qāḍī*, a professor of Arabic, and a person of good reputation (*ᶜadl*) of the city, all with knowledge of Arabic. This was the situation in Saint Louis. In other towns, the commission was composed of the mayor, two residents who knew Arabic, one of whom had to know French as well. In Article 10, the regulation stipulated that the Qurʾānic schools (designated as "private" schools) could not teach students aged 6 to 15 during the regular hours of "public" (French) schools and that teachers in Quranic schools must only admit students in possession of a certificate attesting to their current enrollment in a public school. Whoever opened a school without authorization, or who continued to teach in a school that had been closed by the authorities could be fined 1 to 15 francs. In case of second offense, the punishment was 1 to 15 days of imprisonment.[43]

Moreover, the colonial administration made it difficult to obtain books on Islamic topics; it tried to limit contact between Muslim Africans and their brethren in the East; it restricted pilgrimage to Mecca, killed a number of Muslim scholars, arrested and unjustly imprisoned others, implemented a secular curriculum instead of an Islamic one in the country's public schools—schools built and maintained with the taxes of Muslim subjects, etc.

Many *ᶜulamāʾ* were well aware of these constraints upon Islam. Alhough the political situation might limit the ways in which to respond to it, they nonetheless believed that at the very least their faith demanded that they break with the colonizers, that they denounce a criminal policy whose ultimate aim was to eliminate Islam from the country so that the minds of its people could more easily be colonized. Foremost among the *ᶜulamāʾ* to adopt this attitude of rejection of all forms of collaboration with the colonizer was *Shaykh* Muḥammad Bamba Mbacké, often known as Ahmad Bamba, founder of Senegal's Mouride brotherhood.

CHAPTER FIVE

THE MOURIDE *ṬARĪQA*

The Mouride *ṭarīqa* was founded at the end of the 19th century by *Shaykh* Muḥammad Bamba Mbacké,[44] born in 1270 or 1272 AH (c. 1853 CE) in the village of Mbacké, in Baol.[45] He was taught the Qur'ān by his mother's maternal uncle, Tafsir Mbacké Ndoumbé in Jolof, but his master died before the student had completed the memorization of the Holy Book. Muḥammad Bamba then (*c.* 1865) joined his father, Muḥammad b. Ḥabib Allāh, better known as Momar Anta Sally, who was at that time working with the Tijānī *Shaykh* Maba Diakhou in Salum. He completed his Qur'ānic studies and was introduced to the fundamental Islamic sciences, *ḥadīth*, *tafsīr* (exegesis), *tawḥīd* (theology), and *fiqh* (jurisprudence) by his maternal uncle Muḥammad Bousso, studies he pursued under *Shaykh* Samba Toucouleur Ka, a paternal cousin. He then went to Patar in Kayor to rejoin his father, who had become *qāḍī* and religious consultant to Lat Dior, the Damel of Kayor. In Patar, Muḥammad Bamba studied not only under his father, but also under his father's colleague, *Qāḍī* Mūsā Diakhaté, better known as Madiakhaté Kala.[46] Madiakhaté Kala taught him Arabic and metrics. Muḥammad Bamba also studied philology and logic under the Mauritanian master Muḥammad b. Muḥammad al-Karīm al-Daymānī. Following his studies, Muḥammad Bamba began to teach in his father's school, eventually replacing him on his death in 1299 AH (11 December 1881). However, he only continued as headmaster for one year. Dissatisfied with the task of transmitting knowledge through traditional methods, he turned his attention to Sufi pedagogy.

On reaching manhood, Muḥammad Bamba Mbacké had been initiated to the Qādirī *wird* by his father. This initiation fulfilled a tendency that had been with him since childhood. However, during the lifetime of his father he had been unable to develop this faculty. His father had always emphasized, rightly, the need to maintain and transmit the ancestral cultural heritage of Islamic scholarship. Though he practiced Sufism himself, Momar Anta Sally gave priority to conventional religious teaching and did not permit his son to practice Sufism before he had acquired the indispensable foundation of Islamic science. In any case, once he was on his own, following the death of his father and master, Muḥammad Bamba returned to his home town of Mbacké-Baol. His stay in Mbacké was of short duration, however, as visitors began to flood in to see the young *shaykh* there. This influx was not welcomed by his family, who believed it to be unjustified.

Shaykh Muḥammad Bamba undertook a number of journeys through Senegal and Mauritania. Everywhere he went he would seek out the most important Sufi masters, enrich his scientific and spiritual knowledge, and acquire the books that were still scattered among the many centers of religious studies. It would seem that books dealing with Sufism attracted him most. He obtained copies of Al-Ghazali's *Iḥyāʾ ᶜUlūm al-Dīn* ("The Revivification of the Religious Sciences"), Abū Ṭālib al-Makkī's *Qūt al-Qulūb* ("Nourishment of Hearts"), al-Qushayri's *Risāla* ("Epistle [on Mālikī law]"), and of Sīdī ᶜAlī Ḥarāzim's *Jawāhir al-Maᶜānī* ("Jewels of Meanings"). These works would exert a great influence on his thought.

If the *shaykh* had hoped that his absence from Mbacké would put an end to the influx of aspiring disciples, he was disappointed. If anything, his absence accelerated the movement of people to the town, much to the annoyance of his family. He attempted to isolate himself from the crowd by establishing a spiritual retreat in the wilderness to the North-East of Mbacké, in a place called *Dār al-Salām* (Abode of Peace), where he could nurture the fruit of his recent readings in Sufism. It was not long, however, before visitors discovered him there and disturbed his peace. They became so numerous that, in 1887, he felt obliged to retreat further into the wilderness, to a less accessible place to the north of *Dār al-Salām* which he called *Ṭūbā*, or Touba (Abode of Felicity).

The great influx of visitors was not only an annoyance to the *shaykh*'s family; it also raised the suspicions of the colonial authorities. They sent numerous agents and informers to Mbacké to report on developments there. When Muḥammad Bamba became aware of this, he at first sought to reassure the authorities of his good intentions, telling them that all he sought was a quiet place where he could pursue his pedagogical mission in peace. This would prove to be insufficient. There were a number of people who felt threatened by the popularity of the *shaykh*. These included members of former royal families who saw him as a dangerous rival, seeking to use Islam in order to acquire the traditional powers they had formerly wielded, as well as other *shaykhs* worried by the influence he had acquired over the masses. These adversaries worked to poison the relations between Muḥammad Bamba and the occupying power.

In the mean time, *Shaykh* Muḥammad Bamba was again obliged to move. His settlement in Touba had been swamped by the uncontrolled arrival of new students. The education system he had established there could not cope with the numbers. This time he left for the village of Mbacké in Jolof, the original home of his ancestors, where he settled with his closest disciples—those he was preparing to continue his mission.

No sooner was he settled in Mbacké-Jolof than new false accusations were being made about him by his detractors. The colonial administration had him arrested, on 13 August 1895, and exiled to Gabon, where he remained for seven years. The authorities and their local allies hoped that the exile would cause the disciples of the *shaykh* to disperse. This time it was they who would be disappointed. The trial of exile increased Muḥammad Bamba's prestige and renown across the country and intensified the love and devotion of his disciples for him. When he returned home on 21 November 1902, the excitement generated caused a popular movement far greater than the one which had prompted his exile in the first place. He was again arrested, on 13 June 1903, and deported to Souet al-Ma in Mauritania, where for four years he was placed under house arrest in the Qādirī *zāwiya* of *Shaykh* Sidiyya al-Kabīr.[47] *Shaykh* Muḥammad Bamba was returned to Senegal in 1907 but was nonetheless kept firmly under house arrest, first in Thiène (Jolof) until 1912, and then in Diourbel (Baol) until his death on 19 July 1927.

Undoubtedly, in the recent history of Senegal, no man has been as unjustly persecuted as this *shaykh*. The influx of people towards him was entirely beyond his control and undesired on his part. Yet it was sufficient to kindle the suspicions and enmity of Muslim adversaries and rivals.

As for the colonial administration, it adopted an uncompromising policy of repression in its dealings with the *shaykh* because it was intent on consolidating its control over Senegal. The colonial forces had crushed the traditional centers of power and authority, and now needed to neutralize Islam, which lay at the heart of national resistance. The ultimate aim of the colonial project was to dominate minds, so as to secure in one form or another the long term interest of the colonizing power. Islam stood in the way of this project. After gathering information about *Shaykh* Muḥammad Bamba Mbacké, the colonial authorities came to the conclusion that, despite his sincerity in claiming that he had no interest in worldly concerns, and that he was entirely absorbed in worship of his Lord, that he might obtain His pleasure, he was nonetheless dangerous. He was attracting groups of people, who did not share his ideas, but who were known to have political agendas of their own. Among the *shaykh*'s followers were men who had been in power before the conquest and who were now seeking a means of regaining it. According to the authorities, these men had joined Muḥammad Bamba only to recruit followers, and obtain the moral support necessary to the fulfillment of their political objectives.[48] Moreover, the authorities persisted in their belief that there was a hidden complicity between the *shaykh* and these "disciples". These suspicions were confirmed in their eyes by the fact that Muḥammad Bamba, almost alone among Senegal's *shaykhs*, refused to entertain any form of collaboration with the colonizers and would not voluntarily submit to being kept under surveillance by them. His motto was: "God be witness that I seek no dealings with polytheists".

As for the attitude of *Shaykh* Muḥammad Bamba's rivals among the *ʿulamāʾ* , it can be explained for two reasons. First, they had been unable to articulate a clearly anti-colonial position. They were bothered by the fact that the *shaykh* took just such a position and expressed it in Islamic terms. Their superficial criticism of him could not cover this feeling of malaise. Secondly, and this reason is more troubling, they were deeply disturbed by the fact that many of their own disciples, and even some of their colleagues, were attracted to Muḥammad Bamba. Qādirī and Tijānī *shaykhs* alike are known to have "converted" to his spiritual guidance. One famous Sufi poet gave expression to this transfer of spiritual allegiance in terms of the homelands of the competing *ṭarīqas*:

> I no longer need either Baghdad or Fez,
> On seeing Jolof, I submitted entirely.[49]

Added to these concerns was the troubling fact that *Shaykh* Muḥammad Bamba had received the Tijānī *wird*. According to the conditions under which this *wird* is obtained is the stipulation that it must be retained "until death". For Tijānīs, to abandon this *wird* is tantamount to apostasy. Moreover, Muḥammad Bamba's justification for abandoning the Tijānī *wird* (in his words, the last "foreign" *wird* he would use) implied that he had reached the same spiritual rank as *Shaykh* Aḥmad al-Tijānī and was consequently independent of him. This was particularly troubling for Tijānīs, because of the claim of the founder of the *ṭarīqa* to be the "Seal of the Saints". Like the "Seal of the Prophets", the "seal" of the saints must be the best, and the last, among them.

For all of these reasons, the colonial administration and certain local notables worked hand in hand to suppress *Shaykh* Muḥammad Bamba Mbacké.

> "Members of other Qādirī organizations, and especially members of the Tijāniyya, can be useful agents and informants, though one should never accept their information uncritically. In many cases they are the ones who are motivated either by hate for Muḥammad Bamba's followers, or for reasons of personal gain. It is they who have given the Mourides such an appalling reputation, one that is not necessarily deserved."[50]

Paul Marty, the author of the above lines, was among the most tenacious adversaries of *Shaykh* Muḥammad Bamba and his disciples. It is even highly probable that it was he who commissioned a poem, of mediocre quality, and unlike anything Muḥammad Bamba would have written, which he inserted in his book as proof of the *shaykh*'s utter submission to the colonial authorities towards the end of his life. The poem begins as follows:

Muslims will be well, without sadness,
So long as there is among them an authority,
who repels sadness...![51]

To our mind, this poem is unquestionably the work of wolves in sheep's clothing.[50] If *Shaykh* Muḥammad Bamba had submitted to the colonial administration at the end of his life, why, then, was he not permitted to travel freely through the land like the other religious leaders of the day? How "well" could Muslims be when the greatest of their *shaykhs* was living under house arrest, unable to fulfill his heart's desire—which was to settle in Touba?

Shaykh Muḥammad Bamba's Thought

Shaykh Muḥammad Bamba began writing at an early age. Already while studying under his father, he wrote a poem of 644 verses called *Mawāhib al-Quddūs* based on the *Umm al-Barāhin*, a theological treatise by al-Sanūsī. The young poet stuck closely to the original text, adding only comments to some of al-Sanūsī's ideas. It would seem that his main objective was to facilitate the memorization of the treatise by young people. The doctrines presented by al-Sanūsī, are those which al-Ashᶜarī had defended prior to his adherence to the "People of the *ḥadīth*" school of thought, a school which originated with the ultra-traditionalist imam Aḥmad Ibn Ḥanbal. Prior to his about face, al-Ashᶜarī had in fact been a defender of the metaphorical interpretation regarding divine attributes. This doctrine had been propagated under his name and was taught in many schools, which explains how it has come down to us today. Muḥammad Bamba wrote another poem in his youth, entitled *Mulayyin al-Ṣudūr* (Softening of Hearts) based on al-Ghazālī's *Bidāyat al-Hidāya* (Beginning in the Right Direction). Having lost this poem, he later rewrote it as *Munawwir al-Ṣudūr* (Illuminator of Hearts). Both poems were brought to the attention of his father, who was so pleased at the efforts of his son, that he used them himself for teaching children. Generally speaking, the *shaykh*'s poems relate to a number of themes:

•theology, as in *Mawāhib al-Quddūs*, and *Tazawwud al-shubbān*;

•jurisprudence, as in *al-Jawhar al-nafīs*, and *Tazawwud al-ṣighār*;

•Sufism, as in *Masālik al-jinān*, *Munawwir al-ṣudūr*, and *Maghālīq al-nīrān*;

•religious morals, as in *Nahj qaḍā' al-ḥajj*;

•panegyrics to the Prophet (PBUH).

These works, with the exception of the last category, were based on existing texts. The *shaykh* composed them in order to facilitate their memorization, particularly by children:

> This is to be a present,
> For all of contemporaries who want to memorize it.

The texts on jurisprudence and Sufism were however added to, enriched, with the aim of making the verses clearer and explaining the choice of questions discussed:

> I often add ideas,
> To make the text useful to the mildly intelligent.

While it remains difficult to date his various works precisely, we can say with some certainty that, apart from his panegyrics to the Prophet (mostly composed in exile in Gabon 1895-1902), most of his writings date from before his exile (1870-1895). Among the most important of these can be cited:

•*Mawāhib al-Quddūs* (Gifts of the Most-Holy),

•*Masālik al-jinān* (Paths to Paradise), and

•*Maghālīq al-nīrān* (Padlocks to [shut off] Hell).

The author places great emphasis on *tawḥīd* (theology of God's "oneness"), law, and the necessity of education in fundamentals in order to acquire sound moral and ritual habits. In *Mawāhib al-Quddūs* Muḥammad Bamba says:

> That said, sciences are the best heritage,
> The best benefit God can bring to a servant.
> But *tawḥīd* remains the most prescious treasure for man,

In the tomb and on the Day of Resurrection.
It can replace the other sciences,
But they cannot replace it.

And in *Masālik al-Jinān*:

Tawḥīd is absolutely the best of sciences,
According to consensus,
Then comes *tafsīr* (Qurʾānic exegesis),
Then the *ḥadīth* according to al-Daymānī,
After these three comes *fiqh* (jurisprudence),
No-one can deny this.

Know that science and action
Are surely the means to happiness.
Devote yourselves to it,
And to your purification from all faults,
By following the example of the *Sunna* and of the 'Selected One',[52]
May the Creator bless him and greet him.

Finally, in the *Maghālīq al-nīrān*:

The darkness caused by deviation of faith
Hides the light created by obedience to the Guide.
Whoever forbids you to learn
Has formulated an erroneous prohibition,
For any person who is against instruction
In these times only promotes
Odious innovation.
An action not based on knowledge
Is tainted by error.

Shaykh Muḥammad Bamba's Sufism is best expressed in a poem he wrote at the instigation of his professor of Arabic, *Qāḍī* Madiakhaté Kala mentioned above. In it he says of the Sufis:

Here are the real men whose companion is never unfortunate;
They procure happiness for postulants (initiates-*murīds*).

The Birth of the Mouride Ṭarīqa

We have already seen how *Shaykh* Muḥammad Bamba Mbacké succeeded his father as teacher of the religious sciences and how he only pursued this profession for a brief period before turning resolutely towards Sufi education. After having taken this decision he is reported to have gathered his disciples together to tell them: "Whoever came to me exclusively for the purpose of instruction is free to go wherever he pleases. And whoever wants what I want is invited to follow me and to take my orders."[53] After this solemn declaration most of the disciples left. Only a small group remained. This became the first group of *murīds*. The *shaykh* told these disciples that he had received the order from the Messenger (PBUH) to declare his spiritual mission. This "declaration" features in one of his poems:

> Among the prodigies of Ibn 'Abd Allāh (the Prophet Muḥammad)
>
> Is the good news he brought to his servant (Khadīm al-Rasūl, i.e. Muḥammad Bamba) when he told him: "Declare....

His disciple and hagiographer Muḥammad al-Amīn Diop comments on the term "declare" as follows:

> When, with God's help, he had completely assimilated the inheritance (of the Prophet), through the expansion of his knowledge, his wisdom, his enlightenment and his secrets, so that he was strong enough to take on the burden of supreme sanctity, then (the Prophet) ordered him to invite men to join him and to be initiated by him, to obey his orders and prohibitions.[54]

According to this author, the new *ṭarīqa* was an expression of sincerity, considered as the essence which gives value to religious action and as "the fruit of knowledge and the means of attaining the higher states of spiritual hierarchy; sincerity expresses a state of complete devotion in which the believer dedicates all his movements, his rest, his beliefs, acts, words, and inner and exterior states to God."[55] The means used in these spiritual exercises, the aim of which was to provoke a state of sincerity, were: extreme sobriety in matters relating to food, permanent physical effort, constant maintenance of a state of ritual cleanliness, reduction to a necessary minimum of intercourse with women, and the nearly perpetual practice of *dhikr*.

Shaykh Muḥammad Bamba did not apparently establish his own *wird* until twenty four years after he embarked upon his mission of spiritual education. Until then, he had used, in chronological order, the Qādirī *wird* he had received from his father, the Shādhilī *wird* he had received from a Mauritanian *shaykh*, and finally the Tijānī *wird*—the last "foreign" *wird* to be used by him before he declared his independence from other *ṭarīqas*. In effect, it is during the month of Ramaḍān 1322 AH (1904 CE.), while in Sarsar (Mauritania), that the *shaykh* declared that, like *Shaykh* Aḥmad al-Tijānī before him, he had had a physical encounter with the Prophet (PBUH). The Prophet transmitted to him a new *wird* from God Most-High. This Mouride *wird* goes as follows:

- I ask for God's protection against Satan the damned. I protect (my soul) and protect its descendants for You, against Satan the damned. Lord, I ask for protection against the temptations of devils and against their invasion. (once)
- I seek the protection of perfect divine words against the ills of creatures. (3 times)
- In the name of God, the Merciful, the Beneficent. (once)
- In the name of God, whose name repels all harm on earth and in the sky. He hears all and knows all. (3 times)
- In the name of God, [occurs only] what pleases God, only He brings good.
- In the name of God, [occurs only] what pleases God, only He bars evil.
- In the name of God, all good that reaches you is from Him.
- In the name of God, (occurs only) what pleases God, there is neither means nor force except in God.
- In the name of God, the fully Important, the Almighty, what pleases Him happens.
- I ask God's protection against Satan. (3 times)
- recitation of the "Throne Verse" (2:255). (3 times)
- recitation of Qur'ān 9:128: "Now has come unto you an Apostle from amongst yourselves". (once)

- recitation of Qur'ān 40:44: "My affair I commit to God; for God watches over His Servants.". (once)
- recitation of Qur'ān 9:129: "God is sufficient for me; there is no god but Him, I put my trust in Him alone, He is the Lord of the Throne supreme!". (70 times)
- There is no god but God, and Muḥammad is the Messenger of God, may God bestow blessing and peace upon him and his kin and his companions. (50 times)
- recitation of the "Prayer of the Opening". (100 times)
- There is no god but God. May God bless and greet our lord and master Muḥammad, the illiterate prophet, his kin and his companions, with blessing and greeting, thanks to which You will give me happiness; no misfortune will be able to shatter, and the most perfect pleasantness on Your part which will never be followed by anger. (once)
- O Generous One, O Beautiful One, O Tender One, O Lord of Worlds, Creator, O Donator, O Gentle One, O Generous One, O Useful One, O Most Generous One, O Eternal One, O Creator of life here and in the Hereafter, Master of this world and of the next and of all that separates them.
- recitation of Qur'ān 2:25: "Give glad tidings to those who believe and do good, that their portion is gardens, beneath which rivers flow. Each time they eat the fruits therefrom, they say: "Why, this is what we were fed with before," for they are given things in similitude; and they have therein companions pure; and they abide therein (forever)". (once)
- Praise your Lord, Lord of power, (far from) what they (idolaters) describe. Peace on the messengers and praise God, Lord of Worlds.

The *murīd* is required to recite this *wird* once a day and to read a sixtieth part (*ḥizb*) of the Qur'ān each day if he can. This *wird* was not however imposed by the *shaykh* on anyone. Quite to the contrary, the *shaykh* would say: "Those of you who already have a *wird* and can use it along with this one will be rewarded with a more intense light. The one who cannot practice both must be content with this noble *wird*".[56] Older Mourides will scrupulously practice the *wird*. Yet it does not seem that its regular use is a condition for belonging to the Mouride *ṭarīqa*. Given the difficulty of using it properly, and most people would be unable to fulfill the conditions, it is only given to those who ask for it.

Besides the *wird*, Mourides also frequently recite the panegyric poems their *shaykh*, Muḥammad Bamba, composed to honor the Prophet Muḥammad (PBUH), the most famous of which are: *Mawāhib al-Nāfiᶜ* (Gifts of the Propitious), *Jadhb al-qulūb* (Attracting Hearts), and *Muqaddimat al-amdāḥ* (Introduction to Panegyrics). The *shaykh* encouraged the organization of individual and group recitations as a means of taking the minds of *murīds* off mundane and useless things and focusing them instead on *dhikr* and panegyrics for the Prophet (PBUH). Sessions of group chanting are a regular part of Mouride religious practice and constitute one of its strongest traditions.

The Expansion of the Mouride Ṭarīqa in Senegal

We have already stated that, towards the end of his father's life, *Shaykh* Muḥammad Bamba Mbacké was teaching the Islamic sciences to most of his father's students, as the latter was occupied as *qāḍī* and jurist to *Damel* Lat Dior Diop of Kayor. The *shaykh* must have been successful at this task, since he attracted more students. He acquired a reputation for sobriety, for rejecting worldly things, and for a sincere desire to apply his knowledge. It must be emphasized here that Muḥammad Bamba never turned his back on the teaching of fundamental religious sciences. He repeatedly reiterated that "I have taught the dogma of *tawḥīd* and the rules of ritual cleanliness, fasting, and everything else a responsible man needs to know to all those who have affiliated themselves to me, for the love of God Most-High and Generous."[57] Careful scrutiny of his writings reveals the importance the *shaykh* placed on the propagation of Islamic sciences. He was adamant that their acquisition and assimilation was necessary to the spiritual fulfillment of all Muslims.

However, in much of the literature about the Mourides one can read the claim that the dismissal in 1882 of most of his students amounts to proof that *Shaykh* Muḥammad Bamba preferred Sufism to discursive knowledge, and that this is the source of ignorance among Mourides. In truth however, Sufism cannot be practiced correctly without the underlying sciences necessary to proper devotion. It is not incompatible with the pursuit of religious knowledge. What the *shaykh* was doing was experimenting with an educational system which integrated the teaching of the basic religious sciences to the acquisition of Sufi devotional practices. He was convinced that while the acquisition of massive amounts of knowledge and insight might earn a man the admiration of his companions and colleagues, it would not earn him the pleasure of God unless it was linked to sincere acts in full conformity with the Prophet's *Sunna*.

Most of the *shaykh*'s contemporaries did not even try to understand this pedagogical system. They considered it an innovation that would hinder the classical teaching of Islam—a method which until then had assured the spread of the religion. This conviction was reinforced by the rapid growth of disciples, which occurred immediately following the *shaykh*'s implementation of the new pedagogical system. Everyone from destitute peasants to dethroned royalty flocked to his side. These were people who had never previously shown any interest in learning Islam, and who were not known for their religious devotion. It seems certain that there were among them some who were seeking not to perfect their religion, but rather to attach themselves to a national leader who might help them in recuperating the power and prestige lost to them by colonization. This phenomenon, which, as we have seen, aroused the suspicion and retribution of the colonial authorities, was also a source of anxiety for the inhabitants of the town of Mbacké. Some of them adopted an overtly hostile attitude towards *Shaykh* Muḥammad Bamba's *murīds*, fearing that these elements would eventually dominate the movement.

Shaykh Muḥammad Bamba himself seems at first to have been overwhelmed by the sheer number of new disciples. His first reaction was to try to escape the pressure by isolating himself in spiritual retreats ever deeper in the wilderness, first in Dār al-Salām, then in Touba. He would spend days in these retreats, visiting Mbacké only late at night, to the point that even the most level-headed of his disciples complained about his behavior to his maternal uncle Muḥammad Bousso. The head of the Bousso family asked his distraught nephew how, according to the norms of the *sharīʿa*, he could defend his habit of avoiding poor disciples, who were only looking for a guide to put them on the Straight Path. Muḥammad Bamba replied that if a Sufi, who was struggling to perfect his spiritual state, reveled in the company of people, he ran the risk of being bogged down by them, of becoming imprisoned by their mundane preoccupations. Not only would such a Sufi be unable to exercise a positive influence on his disciples, he might even become an instrument of their will.

The massive influx of new disciples, which forced the *shaykh* to seek refuge in the wilderness beyond Mbacké, enticed the authorities to investigate him and his movement. The authorities were particularly worried that the crowd of *murīds* assembled around the *shaykh* would take up arms in insurrection, and that they would be led in this enterprise, not by the *shaykh* himself, but by the members of the former royal families who had joined the Mouride movement. It was claimed that Muḥammad Bamba was in league with Saër Maty Ba, successor to the Tijānī *jihād* leader Maba Diakhou and declared enemy of the colonial presence, and that he was serving as intermediary between Saër Maty and Tanor Ngoy, the *Teigne* of Baolone, one of the *shaykh*'s disciples, who was also an avowed enemy of the French.[58] This is why the colonial administration placed the Mourides under discrete, yet permanent, surveillance. The faster the movement grew, the more intense the surveillance became. Muḥammad Bamba was subjected to pressure aimed to reduce the number of his followers. He told those of them who did not desire religious instruction and spiritual education to go home. Moreover, he did everything in his power to discourage people from remaining in his entourage. He retreated deep into the wilderness, settling in a place lacking in drinking water and other essential amenities, where daily life was a trial; all this in the hope that those who were not committed to the struggle of the soul against material things would leave.

This spiritual battlefield was none other than Touba, destined to become a great holy city. Muḥammad Bamba's disciples were grouped together in Touba. Children were placed under *Shaykh* ʿAbd al-Raḥmān Lo, one of his famous disciples, for basic Qurʿānic education, while the adults studied the Islamic sciences under the *shaykh*'s brother and lieutenant, Ibrāhīm Mbacké.

Finally, the *shaykh*'s maternal cousin, the famous scholar Mbacké Bousso, was responsible for the administration of the community of disciples. This system was disturbed however by the arrival in Touba of entire families. Most of the new arrivals "were only interested in the person of the *shaykh*", in other words they had not come to learn anything. In 1889 Clément Thomas, Governor of Senegal, ordered the dismissal of Muḥammad Bamba's disciples, but it must be said that the *shaykh* never dismissed a disciple, i.e., someone who had taken the *wird*, but only followers who showed no aptitude for religion and spiritual education.

In one final attempt to isolate himself from the crowd, in 1895, *Shaykh* Muḥammad Bamba left Touba with about 500 of his most sincere *murīds* for the ancestral home of Mbacké-Jolof, about 50 km to the north-east, where he hoped to lay the foundations of the *ṭarīqa*. As for the rest of his followers, they remained in Touba where, in order to stop them from becoming public nuisances, they were required to work and earn an honest living. This set-up failed. The followers were attracted to the *shaykh* by some irresistible force. They refused to do as he ordered, and remain behind and work. They took to the roads of Jolof in search of him. This resulted not only in a serious deterioration of his relations with the traditional political authorities in Jolof, it also sealed his fate in the eyes of the colonial power. He was arrested and exiled to Gabon.

Muḥammad Bamba's exile stemmed for a time the influx of new followers. His absence, however, had a positive effect on the new *ṭarīqa*, to the extent that his educational system could finally be successfully implemented. ᶜAbd al-Raḥmān Lo, Ibrāhīm Mbacké and Mbacké Bousso fulfilled the teaching functions assigned to them by their *shaykh*, while another of the *shaykh*'s cousins, Aḥmad Ndoumbé, was put in charge of the laborers.

The *shaykh*'s return from exile, thanks to God and to the intervention of the Mauritanian Qādirī *Shaykh* Sidiyya Bābā (1869-1924), in 1902 was considered by many Senegalese as nothing short of a miracle, and it gave a new impetus to the Mouride movement. The number of new followers exploded, and he once again found himself at the vortex of an uncontrollable mass phenomenon. This led in short order to a new arrest on 13

June 1903, and deportation to the Sīdiyya *zāwīya* in Mauritania. *Shaykh* Sīdiyya Bābā was considered by the French to be a "reliable man", a friend of the colonial regime. The authorities hoped that by entrusting Muḥammad Bamba to his surveillance that the prestige of the Black *shaykh* would be eclipsed somewhat by that of the Mauritanian masters. It was also hoped that the troubled country (Mauritania was still a contested military zone at the time) might prove fatal to the Senegalese *shaykh*; in fact there was an unsuccessful attempt on his life there. Finally, in the care of great Sufi masters, *Shaykh* Muḥammad Bamba would be able to quench his spiritual and literary thirst safely, without fear of disturbing public order. These in any case are the explanations of his Mauritanian exile provided by his son and hagiographer Muḥammad al-Bashīr Mbacké, author of *Minan al-Bāqī al-Qadīm fī sīrat al-Shaykh al-Khadīm* (The Benevolences of the Pre-Existent Eternal One concerning the Life of *Shaykh* al-Khadīm).[59]

After four years of exile in Mauritania, *Shaykh* Sīdiyya Bābā and a number of prominent Senegalese citizens affiliated to the Mouride *ṭarīqa* intervened in favor of Muḥammad Bamba. The military administrator of Mauritania even wrote to the Governor General of French West Africa requesting the *shaykh*'s return to Senegal, an event which occurred in April 1907. Once again the authorities could only watch with consternation. No sooner had the *shaykh* set foot in Senegal than people came from all over to join his movement. Despite putting him under strict house arrest, the numbers of his followers continued to grow. By the time of his death in 1927, the authorities estimated their number at 70, 000. It is clear however that disciples duly educated in the principles of the *ṭarīqa* numbered less than one seventh of that number. These were the ones who lived in Touba, which remained a center of religious and civic education during this entire period of turbulence. Students aged 15 to 20 were enrolled in courses in theology, metrics, etc., in what was a veritable "little university" under the supervision of a faculty composed of the *shaykh*'s brothers, sons and cousins: Muḥammad al-Muṣṭafā Mbacké, Muḥammad al-Fāḍil Mbacké, Masamba Mbacké, and Mbacké Bousso.[60] The overwhelming majority of Mourides were not educated in this way. Rather, they had a sentimental attachment to the *shaykh* and believed that the translation of this attitude into services and presents for the *shaykh* could dispense them from the necessity of religious instruction. This surely constituted a deviation from the *shaykh*'s own teachings and the consequences of this mistaken belief grew proportionally as the Mouride *ṭarīqa* continued to grow.

We can identify six main aspects of this deviation from Muḥammad Bamba's teachings:

1.The excessive veneration of the *shaykh*, which can reach the level of deification. Rank and file Mourides are convinced that no good or evil can occur without the combined intervention of both God and Muḥammad Bamba. Some, albeit a tiny minority, even believe the *shaykh*'s rank to be superior to that of the Prophet Muḥammad (PBUH).

2.The belief of many Mourides that love and veneration for the *shaykh*, and service to his family are sufficient to insure salvation in the Hereafter.

3.The contempt in which many Mourides hold religious knowledge and the strict observance of ritual practices. These elements within the *ṭarīqa* consider such things as signs of a lack of faith in the capacity of the *shaykh* to insure salvation to all creatures, on condition that they love him and serve his family. Advocates of this attitude invoke verses written by the *shaykh* himself in a poem entitled *Taysīr* (Facilitation):

Any (person) who attaches himself to me is saved
From the troubles of this world and the next.
Any (person) who seeks refuge with me will find happiness
And distance from all evil.

These ill informed Mourides are forgetting that the "attachment" mentioned in the above verse must be understood in the context of the entire poem, which, like many of the *shaykh*'s poems, relates to the merits of education. The term "attachment" is recurrent in his work, and he defines it as the application of his teachings by his *murīds*. Practically speaking, Mourides must learn enough of the religious sciences to be able to worship properly, and must use their learning in conformity with the Qur'ān and the *Sunna*.

4.The exploitation of the unconditional obedience that the *shaykh* demands of his *murīds* for material gains and profane purposes, to the detriment of religious education. Countless men have spent their entire youth in the service of a *shaykh*, without having learnt the first thing about religion. This is in diametrical opposition to the educational ideas of Muḥammad Bamba:

Surely the *murīd*, wherever he may be, never wants

But that which pleases the Clement.

The distinctive trait of the *murīd*

Is his abandonment of a will of his own,

In favor of that of God, who does what He wants.

Whoever wants nothing will receive His kindness.

The *shaykh* never disobeys the Intercessor.

Whoever therefore follows his instruction will profit.

This "master educator", as preached by Muḥammad Bamba, is imbibed with religious knowledge. This knowledge dictates all his acts, and obedience to him is conditional on it. In no case may he place himself in contradiction with the message of the Prophet (PBUH), or acquiesce in its violation, or accept the company of those who persist in flaunting the *Sunna*.

5.The exaggerated importance given to birthright and inherited status, to the point of believing that one's birth alone is sufficient to attain salvation in the hereafter, and entitles one to respect, even veneration, independently of whether one respects the *sharīᶜa* or not. In the Mouride scheme of human relations, the closer one is to the Muḥammad Bamba in terms of genealogy, the more respect one receives. Degree of personal piety does not even enter into the equation. Moreover, belonging to Muḥammad Bamba's family, or clan, is sufficient in the eyes of rank and file Mourides to qualify as "*shaykh*", as "master educator", even if one is absolutely ignorant of religious matters and exclusively occupied by the affairs of this world.[61] This popular attitude is in clear contradiction with an eternal Islamic principle as specified in the Qur'ān: "Verily the most honored of you in the sight of God is [he who is] the most righteous of you. And God has full knowledge and is well acquainted [with all things]" (49:13).

6.A certain lax attitude towards the laws regulating marriage among certain *shaykhs* and their *murīds*. This includes exceeding the legal limit of four wives at a time, and abusive recourse to divorce.[62]

These deviations had already taken hold during the lifetime of Muḥammad Bamba. He was unable to eliminate them for two essential reasons. First, his relative lack of freedom during over thirty years of exile and house arrest. His relations with disciples in this period were filtered through the prison of his circumstances. At times he was able to instruct them. The level, form, and content, of this instruction varied according to the intended audience. The themes addressed to the masses of Mourides had to do with the relative insignificance of this life as compared to the life to come, discipline, work, etc., while the elite were instructed in such things as religious history and Sufism. Some of the disciples who attended these lectures latter transmitted their contents to colleagues who could not attend. As most Mourides were far from the *shaykh*, they were not always able to apply the information they received second or third-hand, though some did manage to conform to the instructions. This is in keeping with the Quranic conception of the belief of the majority: "...Yet most of mankind believe not " (40:59), "Yet most of mankind have has no faith, however ardently you desire it" (12:103). Secondly, the believer is often faced with a choice between personal interest and religious obligation. Again, the majority of believers are not prepared to foreswear their immediate personal interests in favor of religion. They may even be prepared to do the contrary if they cannot reconcile the differences between the two. This is apparently what happened to a good number of Mouride *shaykhs* who, though they were well aware of the disregard of their adherents for the instructions of the master, thought that any attempt to force compliance might cause "massive resignations" from the ranks of the *ṭarīqa*. This would have amounted to a reduction in the work force and in monetary returns for the *shaykhs*, and therefore they did nothing. Thus was one of the fundamental conditions for the proper functioning of the Sufi *shaykh*, "the preference for otherworldly concerns over those of this one", ignored.

The Baay Faal

In discussing the Mouride *ṭarīqa*, one cannot avoid mention of an eccentric group within it, commonly referred to as the "Baay Fall". They claim to be followers of *Shaykh* Ibrāhīm Fall, who was an early follower of *Shaykh* Muḥammad Bamba Mbacké, whom he first met in 1883. According to the *Minan al-Bāqī al-Qadīm*, Ibra Fall was wandering through the land searching for a "guide to take him to God" when he found *Shaykh* Muḥammad Bamba in the village of Mbacké-Kayor. Rather than be content with simple submission to his new-found *shaykh*, Ibra Fall began showing dramatic and excessive veneration for him—surprising even the *shaykh* himself. For instance, it is reported that the new disciple would catch the water from his master's ablution and drink it! In any case, many are those who believe that Ibra Fall is the one responsible for introducing into the movement deviations like excessive veneration, total submission, and relentless work, for the sole benefit of the *shaykh*.

Ibrāhīm Fall was a member of the royal family of Kayor. He was engaged in commercial ventures and had amassed a considerable fortune, which, after his adherence, he proceeded to put at the disposal of his *shaykh*. He became the model of the perfect Mouride. A number of his kin folk and entourage, descendants of the *damel*s and their allies, and especially of families that had had a servile relationship with the royal family, followed in his foot steps. The devotion of the followers of "*Shaykh* Ibra" to their leader was every bit as excessive as the devotion of Ibra Fall to *Shaykh* Muḥammad Bamba. In *Minan al-Bāqī al-Qadīm*, *Shaykh* Muḥammad al-Bashīr Mbacké provides examples of the role that Ibra Fall played in the development of the Mouride brotherhood. He attempted to follow the *shaykh* in exile, and reestablished contact with him. He intervened with the colonial administration to free his *shaykh* of accusations and prove his innocence. He also "sent many gifts to *Shaykh* Ibrāhīm Mbacké (Muḥammad Bamba's brother) because our *shaykh* had recommended to him that he help his family, his kin, friends and brothers in religion. He completed this task with competence. Indeed, I can still remember the heavy loads he sent to Mbacké, his impressive gifts to *Shaykh* Muḥammad Diara (Muḥammad

Bamba's elder brother), whom he supported in the absence of the *shaykh*, his generous donations to the poor migrants who depended on religious support, on the upholding of the divine word, who were members of the *shaykh*'s family and who, with his departure, had lost their only source of livelihood."[63]

From the inception of the Mouride *ṭarīqa*, the Baay Fall, as the followers of Ibra Fall became known, constituted its social and economic core. For instance, they were very active in groundnut cultivation, Senegal's main economic sector since the middle of the previous century. The revenues they obtained from this cash crop were the most important source of funding for the *ṭarīqa* in *Shaykh* Muḥammad Bamba's day, as the Baay Fall would bring the fruit of their work to the *shaykh* or to his lieutenants. Moreover, as a labor force, the Baay Fall were essential to the *ṭarīqa*'s big construction projects, such as the building of the mosque of Diourbel (completed in 1925), the construction of the 45 km long Diourbel-Touba railway (completed in 1931) and the building of Touba's great mosque (completed in 1963).

The Baay Fall are mostly famous for their distinctive behavior. For instance, they refuse to pray or to fast under the pretext that *Shaykh* Muḥammad Bamba dispensed them from these obligations in order that they might work more. This attitude does not seem to have prevailed at the beginning of the movement. In his description of Ibra Fall's village, located near Thiès and now absorbed by the city, Paul Marty (writing before 1917) mentions two mosques, a great one and a small one.[64] Neglect of religious obligations only seems to have taken hold among the Baay Fall in the last few years of their founder's life, in the late 1920s. Today, some Baay Fall go so far as to forbid prayer and fasting in their communities, while others, paradoxically, remain faithful to all the Islamic ritual practices. There can be no question, however, of *Shaykh* Muḥammad Bamba ever having dispensed the Baay Fall from prayer and fasting, two of the five pillars of Islam. He could not have done so simply because it was beyond his authority to do so. Moreover, in a letter written by Muḥammad Bamba to Ibra Fall, the latter is specifically asked to persevere in prayer and fasting. This letter dated from the period of his Gabonese exile (1895-1902). One might be permitted to argue that reality on the ground in the entourage of Ibra Fall was significantly different from what written documents might suggest, and that the Baay Fall movement, even in its infancy, was characterized by abstention from prayer and fasting. This movement was very much a popular, uneducated, movement, consisting of neophytes to Islam. One might expect deviationist behavior. The institutionalization of this behavior however is a much more recent phenomenon. The question remains as to why *Shaykh* Muḥammad Bamba did not denounce companions guilty of such disregard for fundamental Islamic precepts.[65] Perhaps in his estimation of the situation it was his mission to "command what is good and proscribe what is bad", while, ultimately, guidance was God's.

Many Senegalese and foreign scholars, who have written on the Mourides, have failed to clearly distinguish between the majority of Mourides, who observe all the precepts of Islam and apply the teachings of the *shaykh* to the best of their ability, and this faction among them which is concerned only with its internal order and in which various dangerous elements have found a safe haven. They lead a licentious lifestyle completely beyond the control even of the Baay Fall leadership. All Mourides are, then, condemned for laxity because of the Baay Fall. The conflation of the two is sometimes more intentional than this. Adversaries of the Mourides knowingly confuse the definition of the organization as "a human association whose ideological base is constituted by the teachings of Muḥammad Bamba", and the practice of one faction among the Mourides. This, significantly, is the tactic used by enemies of Islam who would like to see this religion take the collective blame for the actions of those who claim to be Muslims but do not practice it adequately. This is clearly aberrant.

CHAPTER SIX

THE LAYENNE *ṬARĪQA*

The name "Laayèene" is derived from the Arabic term *ilāhyyīn*, which means "people of God", or "deists". This designation is inspired by the Qur'ānic verse: "Our people, harken to the one who invites [you] to God, and believe in him" (46: 31) which the Laayèene *ṭarīqa* uses as its motto. In Senegal, the name designates the followers of Libasse Thiaw, better known as Limamoulaye, (from Arabic:*imām Allāhi*="the Imām of (or designated by) God". The Laayèene are chiefly concentrated on the Cap Vert peninsula where the sanctuaries of Yoff and Cambérène are located.

Libasse Thiaw, the founder of the *ṭarīqa*, was born in the fishing village of Yoff, now a suburb of Dakar, *c*. 1843. He lost his father in infancy, and was raised by his mother. He received no instruction as a child, and earned his living fishing, the traditional activity of the Lebu.[66] Towards the age of forty he lost his mother and it seems that the bereavement provoked such a deep psychological, and even psychic, crisis that his family and neighbors believed that he was going insane. He, on the other hand, interpreted the crisis as a sign announcing his divine mission, a mission he declared publicly on 1 Shaʿbān 1300 AH (6 June 1883), a date still commemorated by Laayèenes each year in Yoff.

Some of the inhabitants of Yoff subscribed to Limamoulaye's mission and joined him. This first group of Laayèenes then grew to the point of raising the suspicions of the colonial authorities. The authorities were convinced that this "Imām of God" was recruiting soldiers and collecting arms in order to initiate a *jihād* against them. This conviction persisted despite Limamoulaye's declarations to the contrary: "For our part, we have no need to make *jihād*, I recommend to you *jihād* against the passions of the soul."[67] Some Lebu notables were dispatched to Limamoulaye by the colonial administration. They asked him to disperse his followers and to leave Yoff. At first he was categorical in his refusal to comply with the orders, and said that he would not budge, but he then backed down, dismissed his followers and took refuge in Cambérène, a locality a few kilometers to the East. He was nonetheless arrested in September 1887, and imprisoned for three months on the island of Gorée. When he was freed, he was authorized to return to his home town, and henceforth adopted the most submissive and conciliatory policy in his dealings with the authorities.

This attitude is revealed in his correspondence, such as in the following letter:

To the Director of Native Affairs,

Dakar

I am honored, Director, to come and solicit the terms of your high consideration, to be kind enough to permit me to remove the agricultural village I have established on the heights above Cambérène, and to transport my buildings there to my house in Yoff.

As the Administrator has already taken the census for tax purposes, I promise to pay the dues for all the inhabitants of Cambérène. After having paid these dues, I ask you to permit me to assemble my students in my village of Yoff, and abandon Cambérène.

In Yoff I will submit to all regulations and customs as determined by you. As in Yoff and Ouakam, whatever they do, we will do.

I remain hopeful, Director, that you will receive my request favorably.

Please receive, Director, the assurance of my deepest respect.

Your servant, Limamou.[68]

From 1887 until his death in 1909, Limamou preached the doctrines that would characterize his *ṭarīqa*. He taught his disciples that he was a prophet sent by God to the black race, that he was a saint, master of creatures, and an incarnation of the Prophet Muḥammad. "He who has something to give Muḥammad should give it to me, as I am the addressee."[69] Moreover, he maintained that the belief of Muslims would remain incomplete if they did not believe him. To his wives he is reported as having declared: "I let you know that your old companion Limamou is different from the one you have now, because God has done His will. He commissioned me to call (people) to Him."[70] To a Lebu delegation he claimed that "God has placed me above you and above all creatures."[71]

Limamou's new message was transmitted through a few sermons in Wolof, which Mukhtar Lo, his disciple and hagiographer, translated into Arabic. These Arabic manuscripts were then collected by Abdoulaye Gaye and translated into French by Assane Sylla and Muḥammad Ṣaghīr Gaye. These sermons contain a number of striking innovations:

> "He decreed that all members of his brotherhood, when performing ablution, must wash the small body parts (hands and feet) up to the elbows and knees (...) and required that boys born into the brotherhood be circumcised on the seventh day following birth, and decreed that girls be betrothed on their baptismal day."[72]

He defined the relations between the brotherhood's *shaykhs* and their *murīds* thus:

> "Know that it is the duty of all religious leaders to practice the commandments of God and His Messenger with fervor, and to advise their disciples to do likewise. The *shaykh* must instill in the *murīd* fear of God's wrath, and call him constantly to God, warn him and exhort him to keep clear of evil."[73]

Limamou insisted in his sermons on the necessity of abandoning frivolous activities incompatible with proper religious practice, and especially advocated the renunciation of mundane preoccupations, rigor in the acquisition of possessions, and respect for the rights and duties incumbent on each member of the family:

> "Eat and drink only what you have procured honestly; ride only what you have procured honestly; wear only cloths honestly obtained. In everything you use, rely only on things honestly acquired."[74]

Concerning the fate in the Hereafter of the father who neglects the education of his children, according to Limamoulaye, these children will say:

> "O our God, exact on our father the harm he has done us; he did not give us names from among those of the saints; he did not educate us; he taught us nothing from God's Book. He did not proscribe to us what God has proscribed. He did not make us practice the commandments of God; he gave us complete freedom to do evil. O God, inflict on him the harm he has inflicted on us."[75]

As for the deviant practices which characterized family celebrations:

> Know that funerals (as they are currently practiced) are not licit. Muslim law forbids them (...) It is possible that the dishes served at funerals are unclean, in as much as they may be composed of a mixture of food honestly and dishonestly acquired. This is because some relatives of the deceased, though they do not have the means, will seek to contribute to the meal. They do this through shame, or from fear of being vilified. They will procure food by illicit or doubtful methods. This is because there are some individuals who denigrate those who do not bring an offering, or those who do not attend the funeral service. They say so-and-so did not come, or I did not see so-and-so, or so-and-so came but brought nothing. This is ugly and has nothing to do with Islam.[76]

The attitude of the Senegalese *ʿulamāʾ* with regard to Limamou and his claims has been one of outright rejection, as Limamou himself recognized. The *ʿulamāʾ* reject first of all the foundation of his mission. The Qurʾān clearly states that "Muḥammad is not the father of any of your men, but (he is) the Apostle of God, and the Seal of the Prophets" (33; 40). This means that no subsequent prophecy can be admitted in Islam. There has been consensus about this since the days of the Companions of Muḥammad, and it has always been maintained within Sunni Islam. The *ʿulamāʾ* also reject the idea of incarnation and consider it to be foreign to Islam.

On the other hand, a well known *ḥadīth* included in Abū Dāwūd's compilation, and considered as acceptable by *ḥadīth* specialists, because it conforms to the spirit of Islam, predicts the arrival, at the beginning of each Muslim century, of a reformer (*mujaddid*) who will rectify the deviations and deformations thathave slipped into Islamic beliefs and practices. It does not seem that this *ḥadīth* precludes the simultaneous appearance of several such reformers in different parts of the Muslim world. In any case, the credibility of such reformers rests with the strict compliance of their teachings and acts with the precepts of the Qur'ān and the *Sunna*. In other words, they cannot contradict the established consensus within the *Umma*, especially in matters relating to dogma. The Senegalese *ʿulamā'* have not been insensitive to the desire of Limamoulaye to reform those Lebu customs and traditions that are contrary to Islam. However, they cannot admit a doctrinal reform that flies in the face of a fundamental Quranic teaching about the finality of prophecy with Muḥammad. Yet the theoretical rejection of what they consider to be a heresy has not been translated into practical opposition to the Laayèene movement. The Laayèene continue to grow in numbers and to develop as a Muslim community. This growth has less to do with new conversions than with steady demographic progression within the initial community.[77]

CHAPTER SEVEN

THE BROTHERHOODS IN CONTEMPORARY SENEGALESE SOCIETY

A study of the role the brotherhoods play in Senegalese society requires a critical assessment of the vertical and horizontal relations which structure these organizations and of the multiple impacts of their cultural, social, economic, and political activities. Only after the analysis of all these parameters can we begin an informed discussion of the matter. If it is the cardinal rule of Islamic jurisprudence that an exact conception of an object is the prerequisite to a fair judgment of it; then the more exact our conception is, the fairer will be our judgment.

Relations within Brotherhoods

Every *ṭarīqa* has an internal structure which binds its members to each other and which constitutes its primary strength...or weakness. If the structure is coherent, it will foster strong social cohesion and will create real solidarity between brothers. This will give the brotherhood a greater chance of longevity, and of having an enduring and profound influence on the affairs of the nation and on society generally.

Ṭarīqas are pyramidal organizations. At the apex is the Caliph, the supreme authority of the community. In Senegal he is often designated as "Caliph-General". The next rank is occupied by *muqaddams* ("supervisors" or "lieutenants"), or *shaykhs* ("elders" or "masters"). They are confirmed in their leadership positions and are authorized to initiate new members. At the base are the constituent masses of disciples or adherents, designated as *murīds* ("aspirants"), or *taalibés* ("students").

The title of Caliph-General was first attributed by the colonial authorities, and is really used only for the Mouride and Laayèene brotherhoods. The various Qādirī and Tijānī organizations are each under the authority of their own Caliphs and are virtually independent of each other, recognizing no single supreme national authority. Some of the Qādirī groups, such as that of *Shaykh* Saᶜd

Būh in Thiès, and of *Shaykh* Maḥfūz in Casamance, are affiliated to the *zāwiya* of Nimzat (Mauritania), where the equivalent of the Caliph-General, a descendent of *Shaykh* Muḥammad al-Fāḍil, resides. The other main Qādirī group recognizes the supreme authority of the Kunta Caliph in Ndiassane. The various Tijānī organizations, such as the Sy of Tivaouane, the Niasse of Kaolack, the Seck of Thiénéba, the Ba of Médina-Gounasse and others, recognize the supreme authority of the mother *zāwiya* in Fez (Morocco) and of the direct descendants of *Shaykh* Aḥmad al-Tijānī, at least in theory.

The Caliph has nearly the same functions in all the brotherhoods. He represents the deceased founder of the *ṭarīqa*; he is the main custodian of its corporate interests, and the supreme arbiter in cases of internal conflict. In theory, the Caliph must possess profound religious knowledge, must be devout in worship, and must lead an ascetic life. He should surpass all his peers in these qualities. In practice, the Caliphate is an hereditary function in all of Senegal's brotherhoods. This goes against the founding principles upon which the Sufi *ṭarīqas* were established but it corresponds to traditional patterns of transmission of temporal authority in that country. Spiritual power, and legitimacy, is assimilated to material property, and is inherited by birth-right. This means in effect that whoever accedes to supreme authority within a *ṭarīqa*, irrespective of the degree of his religious knowledge, piety and sobriety, is automatically accorded all the prerogatives, privileges and respect due the rank.

The Caliph is usually supported in his duties by some form of consultative council composed of eminent *shaykhs* or *muqaddams*. They constitute the intellectual elite of the brotherhood, and are known for the extent of their scholarship and their impeccable moral stature. This inner council participates in the decision making process and supports the Caliph's initiatives. Matrimonial links play an important part in consolidating relations among members of these governing elites, and in creating an internally cohesive *ṭarīqa* organization. Caliphs habitually marry the daughters of leading members of the inner council and vice versa. These matrimonial arrangements are then renewed, generation after generation, creating a tight network of moral and material interests, which, when added to the common religious purpose, promotes the social, economic, and political, solidarity of the *ṭarīqa*. Moreover, the example of this matrimonial practice at the summit of the organization is repeated in its lower echelons as well. This matrimonial practice seems to be inspired by the *Sunna* of the Prophet (PBUH). In effect, the Prophet Muḥammad married ᶜĀᵓisha, the daughter of his companion and first successor (*khalīfa*), Abū Bakr, and Ḥafṣa, the daughter of his companion and second successor, ᶜUmar b. al-Khaṭṭāb. Moreover, he married his eldest daughter Fāṭima to his cousin ᶜAlī b. Abī Ṭālib, and two younger daughters, Ruqayya and Umm Kalthūm, to ᶜUthmān b. ᶜAffān; both of these companions later succeeded to the Islamic Caliphate. The Prophet also married Umm Ḥabība, daughter of the powerful Umayyad patriarch Abū Sufyān b. Ḥarb and sister of Muᶜāwiya, the first Umayyad Caliph. Moreover, all of these matrimonial links involved different members of a same clan, the Quraysh.

The next rank in the *ṭarīqa* hierarchy is constituted of a relatively large number of *shaykhs* who are responsible for supervising and instructing ordinary members, *murīds*, or *taalibés*. They serve as intermediaries between the popular masses of adherents and the Caliph and his entourage. They also fulfill the role of regional representative of the central administration, transmitting instructions and implementing decisions from above, and preparing written or oral reports on developments in their area. They often have great freedom to initiate action on their own, organizing activities and propaganda campaigns for instance, so long as these serve the greater interest of the *ṭarīqa*.

Ordinary disciples may fulfill a number of roles within the *ṭarīqa*. The most ambitious or lucky ones work in the entourage of the Caliph, where they serve him in his public or private functions, in the hope of receiving spiritual instruction, and of obtaining God's pleasure in the Hereafter. Other disciples, the unlucky ones, will be put to work in the brotherhood's fields, where they might spend years cultivating peanuts or grain for little spiritual or material compensation. Working conditions in these rural communities are always harsh. Finally, there are urban disciples, who are in contact mostly with the Caliph's representatives -

though they might visit the Caliph from time to time in organized groups.[78]

The education disseminated by the *ṭarīqas* invariably recommends a completely submissive attitude towards the *shaykh* on the part of disciples, "like a corpse in the hands of the mortician", according to a famous saying. Disciples must avoid any form of disobedience in their public and private lives. Rural disciples, living under the immediate supervision of their *shaykh* or his foreman, follow his instructions to the letter. Urban disciples, especially the educated and the well-off, are less submissive. The most wealthy and influential among them will avoid the intermediary of a *shaykh* and maintain direct contacts with the Caliph. Some of these "lay" members might even become more influential within the *ṭarīqa* than the *shaykhs* of its inner council, offering extraordinarily generous gifts for instance, or providing inestimable services in the *ṭarīqa*'s dealings with the outside world.

Relations between Brotherhoods

We have already discussed the conflict between the Qādirīs and the Tijānīs in Futa Toro which characterized the second half of the 19th century. Until then the Qādiriyya had been the only Sufi *ṭarīqa* present in Senegal. The Tijāniyya then burst forth on the religious scene with unprecedented vigor, at times equivalent to a veritable invasion. In effect, like all new converts, the first Tijānī proselytes were passionate and extreme in their beliefs, and especially in the belief that their *ṭarīqa* was superior to all others and that it should serve as basis for the creation of an Islamic state. It is this extremism that provoked an intellectual and physical reaction on the part of Qādirī *shaykhs*. In *al-Ḥaqq al-mubīn*, *Shaykh* Mūsā Kamara explains the nature of the differences which set Qādirīs and Tijānīs apart in Futa Toro and, as a Qādirī, he defends the positions of his own brotherhood.[79] He nonetheless describes the multiple dimensions of the conflict and the consequences it had on attitudes at the time. For instance, people would refuse to pray behind an imam who was not affiliated to their *ṭarīqa*. Also, disciples of one *ṭarīqa* would refuse to practice certain rituals specific to it in a mosque belonging to another *ṭarīqa*. The Tijānīs, in conformity with the conditions relating to the use of their *wird* (discussed above), refused to visit non-Tijānī saints, whether living or dead. Whereas the prohibition against visiting the tombs of dead saints should cause no problems, the prohibition against visiting living saints had the effect of depriving the faithful of the teachings and prayers of pious people. It was also contrary to the principle of Islamic brotherhood as established in the Qur°ān: "Surely believers are brothers" (49:10) and as confirmed by the Prophet (PBUH), who said: "Believers are like buildings which support one another". At the time, this exclusionary Tijānī attitude had the effect of dividing Senegalese Muslims amongst themselves, which could only facilitate their conquest by colonial forces. It must be stressed here, however, that Senegalese Tijānīs today no longer adhere so formally and intransigent to this precept of their *ṭarīqa*.

In commenting on this Tijānī prohibition, *Shaykh* Mūsā Kamara cites his master, *Shaykh* Saᶜd Būh, according to whom *Shaykh* Aḥmad al-Tijānī only meant by this that the disciples who had migrated and found refuge with him should rely on him alone for their spiritual education. A disciple can only fully benefit from his master's guidance if he is entirely given over to him. A disciple who is not entirely given over to a master, on the other hand, should be free to seek guidance in religious matters from any competent person. *Shaykh* Saᶜd Būh's accommodating attitude towards the teachings of *Shaykh* Aḥmad al-Tijānī was not considered valid by contemporary Tijānī *shaykhs*. They went so far as to declare that the Tijānī *wird* received from *Shaykh* Saᶜd Būh, even if it was being used to the exclusion of any other, was null and void as this *shaykh* was simultaneously bestowing the Qādirī *wird*. The Tijānī *shaykhs* were at least remaining true to their beliefs in their dispute with the Qādirīs. If one believes one's *wird* to be the absolute best, what use does one have of any other. The best *wird* is the one which allows the Sufi to fulfill his aspirations and progress along the path. Anything else is a detour. The Qādirīs, however, interpreted the Tijānī rejection of *Shaykh* Saᶜd Būh's legitimacy as an affront to the spiritual authority of one of their greatest masters. Reconciliation between the two *ṭarīqas* was thus delayed.

These sectarian tensions between Senegal's Sufis were exacerbated by the rise of a third major player on the religious scene, the Mouride *ṭarīqa*, the first specifically West African *ṭarīqa* to emerge. Relations between *Shaykh* Muḥammad Bamba Mbacké and the Qādirī *shaykhs*, and especially with the Sidiyya *zāwiya*, were excellent. Muḥammad Bamba's forefathers had been Qādirīs, and links with that *ṭarīqa* were solid. Until *Shaykh* Muḥammad Bamba declared his independence from "foreign" *ṭarīqas*, it was commonly assumed that his movement was a local branch of the Qādiriyya. Even after this event the Qādirī *shaykhs* continued to regard Muḥammad Bamba and his disciples with favor, and relations between the two *ṭarīqas* remain excellent to this day. Once again, matrimonial alliances have played a major role in consolidating relations between the two brotherhoods. *Shaykh* Muḥammad Muṣṭafā Mbacké, Muḥammad Bamba's eldest son and first Caliph of the Mourides, married ᶜĀᵓisha Kunta, daughter of the Qādirī *shaykh*, Bou Kunta of Ndiassane, while Muḥammad Muṣṭafā's daughter Āminata Mbacké married into the Kunta family. It seems that the Mourides benefited most from friendly relations with the Kunta. When *Shaykh* Bou Kunta died in 1914, *Shaykh* Muḥammad Muṣṭafā Mbacké went to Ndiassane to present his father's condolences; a group of Qādirī disciples used the occasion to transfer their allegiance to the Mourides.

Early relations between the Mourides and the Tijānīs were, on the other hand, rather tense. Mourides invaded the religious scene in the early 20th century with the same fervor and dynamism as the Tijānīs had in the mid-19th. The fact that their founding *shaykh* was a local prodigy reinforced their belief in the superiority of their *ṭarīqa*. The Tijānī attitude towards them went rapidly from benign indifference, to scorn and contempt, and then to open hostility. Mourides responded by loudly proclaiming the superiority of their *shaykh* over all others and by insulting those who stood in their way. Conversion of a large number of Tijānīs to the Mouride *ṭarīqa*, early on, poisoned the relationship further. Those who opposed the Mourides complained to the colonial authorities about this behaviour and were given authorization to chase Mourides from their communities. This marked the beginning of the violent repression of the Mouride movement.

Mourides were beaten, their fields and houses set on fire, and they ended up migrating towards their *shaykh*, who because of this massive influx was sent into exile.

Relations between the Tijāniyya and the Mourides reached their deficiency following the death of *al-Ḥājj* Mālik Sy in 1922. His eldest son and successor to his *zāwiya* in Tivaouane, Abū Bakr Sy, announced his intention to go to Diourbel to visit *Shaykh* Muḥammad Bamba Mbacké, still under house arrest in a suburb of that town. The latter was pleased at the prospect and made arrangements to receive his guest with the highest honors. At the last minute, Abū Bakr Sy canceled his visit because he feared it would be seen as a sign of affiliation or alliance on his part. He probably never realized the full magnitude of the disappointment the cancellation caused. The breach at the summit between the two *ṭarīqas* widened enormously as a consequence.

Since that time normalization of relations between the two *ṭarīqas* has been hindered by a persistent spirit of mutual suspicion and apprehension. Dispite the best efforts of *Shaykhs* Muḥammad al-Fāḍil Mbacké and ᶜAbd al-ᶜAzīz Sy, old prejudices live on.[80] The average Tijānī believes that Mourides are ignorant, fanatical and negligent in their religious observances, whereas the average Mouride considers the Tijānīs to be pretentious hypocrites. It is clear that neither of these judgments is justified. The *shaykhs* of both communities on the other hand tend to treat each other according to the principle of Islamic brotherhood because, for the most part, they are educated in religious matters and have turned their backs on mundane concerns. Moreover, they usually show a sincere desire to apply the principles they have been imbued with, and which define, Islam as a religion of harmony and understanding, not of dissension and bickering. They know that a *ṭarīqa* is supposed to be a means, not an end, and that one should not sacrifice the end in favor of the means. Moreover, they are keenly aware that solidarity, cooperation and mutual aid have permitted Islam to triumph over its opponents, and that the rapid progress of the religion would not have been possible, had its leaders not abided by its core principles and values. Tijānī and Mouride *shaykhs* will therefore cooperate closely with each other. Many Mouride *shaykhs* have sent their children to Tijānī *shaykhs* for Islamic instruction. Such is the case of the Mourides who studied under Tijānī *Shaykh* ᶜAbd Allāh Cissé, whose school in Diamal was a powerful center of Islamic culture, and conversely of the Tijānīs who studied under the Mouride *Shaykh* Muḥammad Dème in Diourbel.

The more educated are the *shaykhs* of any given *ṭarīqa*, the more likely it is they will maintain friendly relations with each other based on brotherly cooperation in the universal spirit of Islam. Inversely, the more interest a *shaykh* has in material concerns, the more likely it is he will behave in a sectarian manner. The colonial administration soon discovered this and used it to their own advantage by setting *shaykhs* up one against the other. It forged alliances with Qādirī families in Futa Toro in order to fight the Tijānī *jihād*. It then used Tijānīs to collect information about the Mourides, and Mourides to spy on their own *ṭarīqa* and others as well. There have been numerous attempts to improve relations between Senegal's various brotherhoods, and between the Tijānīs and the Mourides in particular. These have not been entirely successful, mostly because of the hold that material interests have on certain leaders within these religious institutions. The masses of followers, despite their ignorance and fanaticism, constitute nonetheless the social basis of the *ṭarīqas*. They have in fact been able to dictate their collective will to their *shaykhs*, and have forced them to uphold sectarian interests at the expense of improved inter-brotherhood relations. This can be demonstrated by observing the reactions of disciples to initiatives of this nature. Any *shaykh* who attempts to establish close, unconditional, relations with Muslims from other brotherhoods will see his *taalibés* leave him, and consequently his influence diminish. On the contrary, any *shaykh* who exaggerates the importance of his *ṭarīqa*, and publicly proclaims its superiority, will immediately gain in prestige. The effects of the pressure which the popular masses exert on the *shaykhs* is revealed in the contradictory attitudes one can observe at public religious festivals. *Shaykhs* from different *ṭarīqas* habitually invite each other to attend the ceremonies and commemorations they organize. On these occasions the host will invariably thank his distinguished guests from other brotherhoods for honoring him with their presence, congratulate them for helping to fulfill God's plan, then turn to address the crowd, telling it insistently that truth lies in attaching oneself to the right *ṭarīqa*.

It is because of contradictions such as this one, that Senegal is today the only country in the world where one part of the population can celebrate the *'Id al-Fiṭr*,[81] while the other part waits, where some Muslims continue to fast ,while others judge that the month has come to an end. In Senegal one can hear phrases like: "Today the Tijānīs will break the fast, and tomorrow it will be the turn of the Mourides". More unusual yet, this condition can even prevail within a single family, one spouse fasting and the other not, each following the directives of their respective *ṭarīqas*. This just goes to show that inter-brotherhood marriages, though more common now than in the past, have not yet resulted in improved relations and coordination between the brotherhoods. Such marriages, dictated by objective considerations, are in fact more common among the Sufi leadership, the urban disciples and the educated, than among the illiterate rural masses, which again is an indication of the pressure the masses are able to exert on the system as a whole.

In some Senegalese towns and cities there are distinct Tijānī and Mouride mosques and cemeteries. This does not stop individual worshippers from freely attending the mosque of their choice, but it means that specific Sufi rituals, such as the *waẓīfa* for instance, are only permitted in mosques run by the appropriate *ṭarīqa*. As for separate cemeteries, problems arise when a person with family in both brotherhoods has to be burried. In such a case a mixed cemetery must be found in a city where segregation is not practiced. Sometimes, even then, each group of bereaved will want to chant the specific litany of its own *ṭarīqa*, resulting in a very un-Islamic cacophony. Moreover, Mourides wherever they may live in Senegal will want to be buried in Touba, whereas the small Tijānī community of that city, of ethnic Toucouleur origin, will not bury its dead there. More curious yet, this community even refused to attend Friday prayer in Touba's great mosque until the Mouride authorities of the city told it that its attitude would no longer be tolerated.

In the end, it seems as though the multiple genealogical, cultural, social, economic, and political, links, which the different brotherhoods have forged with each other over the years, have played a positive role in stabilizing inter-brotherhood relations at the summit. As for rank-and-file members, kinship, membership to the same political parties, trade unions and professional associations, partnerships, etc., are the stabilizing elements which prevent sectarian tensions from coming to a head. Overall, they help explain the participation of members of diverse *ṭarīqas* in the religious ceremonies organized by a specific *ṭarīqa*, and the fact that visits to Sufi centers are often attended by people with other Sufi affiliations.

The Brotherhoods and Culture

The founders and propagators of Senegal's brotherhoods were all teachers, and used teaching to achieve their aims. They were especially keen to prepare their own children to succeed them in their mission, and devoted a lot of attention to their education. They established Quranic schools, called *daara*, where children would learn the Holy Book by rote before embarking on the study of the Islamic sciences. Students who graduated from these schools would set up similar schools in their home towns or villages. This is the way religious instruction progressed throughout Senegal until the onset of colonization. The French administration saw the Arabic Quranic school as a serious rival to its own system of secular French-language education and implemented measures to curb it, as we have seen. These repressive measures however failed.

The great *shaykhs* were committed to Islamic education. However, the educational system they established within the brotherhoods, and which survived intact until Senegal's independence in 1960, was characterized by a very traditional pedagogy and a restricted curriculum. As of age 7, children were required to memorize the entire Qur'ān. This might take anywhere from four to ten years, depending on individual ability. After this, students would study the fundamental texts of Malikī *fiqh*: the *Risāla* and Khalīl's *Mukhtaṣar*, al-Akhḍarī's treatise on logic, the *Sullam*, grammar through *Mulḥat al-Iʿrāb*, *Lāmiyyat al-Afʿāl* and the *Alfīyya*, the *Tafsīr al-Jalalayn* in Quʾānic exegesis, the *Muʾallaqāt* and the *Maqāmāt* in Arabic literature, and al-Sanūsī's works on *tawḥīd*. This program would take three or four years to complete. The merit of this educational system lies in the mastery the students would acquire over the texts they were learning, even if these were few in number. Though the texts were in Arabic, students would be instructed in Wolof, their mother tongue, and would concentrate on one or two subjects, assimilate them completely, then move on to others. Originally, mosques were the locus of education. Masters and students would meet in them following early afternoon prayer and would hold class until about 5 p.m. Some masters also held class in the morning.

Since independence the brotherhoods have experienced change and renewal. The very traditional educational system described above, with religious knowledge being transmitted through rote memorization of established texts, has not been maintained. It should be noted that the system was already under severe strain in the preceding period. This is because the Caliphs who acceded to supreme authority at the head of the *ṭarīqas* were confronted with obligations and duties rather different from those of their pioneering fathers. Mostly, they had little time to fulfill the educational role for which their fathers had prepared them Increasingly, they delegated the task of teaching to *shaykhs* whose level of Islamic scholarship was unquestionable. In theory, the *ṭarīqa* was responsible for providing for the sustenance and material needs of these master teachers. In practice however, student labor became the economic mainstay of teachers. Because of the difficulty of earning a living, some masters began to neglect their teaching duties, while students, in protest, began to boycott classes.

Moreover, students were beginning to consider the traditional educational system as archaic and ill-adapted to their desire for access to a vaster and more modern Islamic culture. It was about this time, in the early 1960s, that *shaykhs* began sending their own children, as well as those of their principal disciples, to pursue higher education in the great universities of the Arab world, establishments like Cairo's al-Azhar, the Qayrawīyīn in Fez, al-Zaytūna in Tunis, and the University of Medina (Saudi Arabia).

On returning from these Islamic universities, students continued to foster greater and closer links with the Arab world, enticing other Senegalese students to go there in search of a modern education, even in the non-religious sciences. These graduates from Arab universities lead a broad cultural and educational campaign throughout Senegal in order that the wider population might also benefit from their experience abroad.

Thus a second network of Islamic education was established in Senegal. This network was composed of schools opened and run by the new generation of teachers who had been trained in the Middle East. The schools were modeled on the modern Arab system and offered the same curriculum. Though many of these new schools received moral support from the *shaykhs*, they generally depended for their day-to-day running and upkeep on tuition fees. As the parents of the vast majority of students were poor, the fees were low, to the point of being insufficient to cover costs. Yet despite the financial precariousness of the system, the network expanded. After the success of primary schools, secondary schools and institutes of higher education were established. Several institutions distinguished themselves within this network of modern Islamic education:

- The *Islamic Studies Institute* of Diourbel was founded in 1958 by *Shaykh* Aḥmad Mbacké.[82] It has a primary and a secondary program, has affiliate sections in Dakar, Kaolack, Louga, Touba, and Mekhé, and has an enrollment of 4, 090 students under the supervision of a faculty composed of disciples of its founder. Some of its graduates have gone on to higher education in the Arab universities of the Persian Gulf, in Qatar especially.
- The *Tafsir Aḥmad Ba High School*, founded in 1968, is administered by the *Fédération des Associations Islamiques du Sénégal* (FAIS). It has a primary, middle and secondary program. It is a modern institution which teaches both religious and secular subjects, though with a predominance of the former. 263 boys and 77 girls are currently enrolled. Registration fees amount to 3 500 francs CFA per year plus a

further monthly room and board fee of between 3 500 and 5 000 francs CFA.

- The *Al-Azhar Institute* in Ndame, near Touba, was founded in 1974 by *Shaykh* Muḥammad al-Murtaḍā Mbacké.[83] It has a primary, middle and secondary program, has affiliate sections in Bambey, Kaolack, Saint Louis, Thiès and Bignona. Its 39 627 students are taught by a faculty composed of Senegalese as well as of Egyptian professors sent by al-Azhar University in Cairo. Graduates of the Institute have the option of pursuing studies at its prestigious namesake in Egypt and scholarships to this end are made available.
- The *Shaykh Abdallah Niasse Institute* in Kaolack was founded by the family of the late *shaykh*.[84] It has all three levels of study and includes scientific disciplines as well as the religious and literary ones. Many Senegalese students as well as students from elsewhere in West Africa study there.
- The *Islamic Institute* of Louga was opened on 17 October 1987. It was the brainchild of *Shaykh* Abbas Sall,[85] and was built with the financial backing of the Kingdom of Saudi Arabia. Since its foundation, this institute has become a Saudi institution completely financed by that country and run by a Saudi staff with the help of a senegalese board of professors and civil servants. Students no longer pay tuition fees, and the best of them can get scholarships to study at the Islamic University of Medina. The Islamic Institute of Louga is the largest in terms of facilities and may eventually grow into a full-fledged Islamic University.

These institutions of Islamic education do not practice any form of sectarian discrimination when it comes to admission policies. Any Muslim, regardless of Sufi affiliation, can enroll. In theory this should mean that these schools should be playing a role in the religious *rapprochement* of Muslims. However, in practice, parents prefer to register their children in institutions affiliated to their *ṭarīqas*. Of the five institutions listed above, only the last-named has a secure financial foundation. The first four, on the other hand, share a number of problems:

1. *Meagerness of resources*

These schools are dependent on tuition and related fees paid by the parents of their students. Fees must be kept very low as the clientele is generally very poor. As a result the schools are chronically underfunded and basic amenities are lacking. They are also unable to attract top caliber teachers as they are unable to offer them appropriate salaries. Well-off Muslims rarely patronize these establishments. On the contrary, they are more likely to send their children to private Catholic schools in the belief that they will receive a better education. The great *shaykhs* of the *ṭarīqa* hierarchies, despite their very real influence, do not support these schools. They do not organize fund-raising campaigns for them, nor do they recommend that their more affluent disciples enroll their children in them. Up until now they have not put any pressure on Senegal's political and administrative networks to support these establishments.

2. *Inability to pursue higher education*

In recent years it has become increasingly evident that degrees from these institutions can no longer lead to the pursuit of studies in Arab universities. The scholarships and grants which used to be made available to Senegalese students by universities such as Al-Azhar and those of the Persian Gulf have been terminated. This has caused serious despair among students currently enrolled, and has undermined new enrollments. The feeling that studies in Senegal's institutes of Islamic studies constitute a dead end is reinforced by the extremely poor prospects of the job market. In effect, the only possibility of employment for graduates seems to be the very institutes they graduated from. Yet here too the capacity of these establishments to absorb new teachers is limited due to stagnant or declining enrollment. And salaries are very low.

3. *Lack of endowments*

The first four institutes lack the capacity to self-finance their activities. They do not have the *waqf* (endowments in perpetuity, unalienable property) which traditionally supported Islamic educational institutions in the past. Nor do they have the corporate financial endowments essential to the operation of modern private universities. The various *ṭarīqas*, for their part, have made no attempt to set up financial institutions in support of their educational projects, though they have the moral authority and the material means to do so. Perhaps the reason for this failure lies once again in the triumph of personal over public interest. Many powerful *shaykhs* would rather invest the *ṭarīqa*'s profits in ventures in which they stand to gain personally than in projects which would benefit the *ṭarīqa* as a whole. Critics have compared *ṭarīqas* to cash cows, and badly managed ones at that, where the pasture is common property but the milk is for personal consumption. The unsustainabilty of the system is becoming increasingly apparent.

4. *Lack of recognition of diplomas*

The Senegalese state only partially recognizes Islamic schools. They are authorized to operate freely and to dispense education, and to a degree they are even subsidized by the state. But the state has always refused to recognize the diplomas they bestow. What this means is that graduates of these institutions cannot hope for employment in the public sector, as teachers in public schools for instance, nor can they be admitted to Senegal's state universities.

The organization of public conferences is another cultural activity in which the brotherhoods are frequently involved. Such conferences are very popular and usually have to do with the necessity of being good Muslims and of remaining true to the *ṭarīqa*. They are usually organized on weekends, or on religious or national holidays. The birthday of the Prophet (PBUH), on the 12th of Rabīᶜ al-Awwal, is a very popular date for these events but they punctuate the entire calendar. The larger ones are covered by the national media and the great *shaykhs* use them as platforms to address their disciples.

One of the most important contributions of the religious brotherhoods to culture is the rich and varied corpus of literature which the founding *shaykhs* and their successors bequeathed. They are composed on the one hand essentially of didactic poems on grammar, law or theology, and on the other of beautifully composed panegyrics to the Prophet (PBUH).[86] This last category of poetry plays a prominent role in the singing and chanting sessions which are major public socio-cultural events. These often nocturnal sessions have spiritual, psychological and social dimensions and deserve to be properly studied. They not only serve to bind disciples to their spiritual guide but to each other as well. They are also concrete, visible, public manifestations of a disciple's affiliation to a particular *ṭarīqa*, and are therefore useful social functions. All a disciple needs to do to incur the favor or esteem of his entourage is recite one of the panegyric poems specific to his *ṭarīqa*. His brothers will then commiserate with him to the extent their sincerity will allow. If he then needs a special service from one of them, he has admirably prepared the way! Disciples will also use these poems privately, to console themselves of life's many hardships or to procure spiritual energy before an undertaking. In effect, ordinary disciples are firm believers in the spiritual omnipresence of the authors of these poems. In some Senegalese *ṭarīqas*, these songs are the first sound an individual will hear at birth and they will accompany him to his last resting place. It is generally believed that learning them is an essential part of the education of any disciple.

Poets among the disciples of the founding Sufi masters translated some of their Arabic poetry into the national language, namely Wolof. Two such poets, Serigne Mbaye Diakhaté and Serigne Mūsā Ka, have each bequeathed to us a compilation of Wolof poems dealing mostly with the teachings and writings of *Shaykh* Muḥammad Bamba Mbacké.[87] The Wolof language is widely used in order to popularize religious knowledge and facilitate its acquisition by illiterates.

One last major contribution of *ṭarīqas* to Senegalese culture is in the arts of the book: calligraphy, the making of leather bindings and cases, etc. The Qur'ān is central to all of Islamic culture and the crafts related to its production and preservation in book form have been developed into special arts. The Mourides especially have developed these arts. An established tradition dictated that each *ḥāfiz* ("custodian" of the Qur'ān, one who has committed it to memory) should produce at least one manuscript copy of the Holy Book to offset its scarcity in the days before printing.[88] As part of their mission to spread and deepen the faith, some *shaykhs* recruited scribes of quality and good reputation and set them to work producing beautiful copies of the Qur'ān. At the same time, another group of artisans specialized in the making of leather Qur'ān casings decorated with original designs in Indian ink. In Touba especially, thousands of copies of the Qur'ān have been preserved in exactly this way in the private collections of *shaykhs*.[89]

The Brotherhoods and the Economy

The brotherhoods contribute most to the economic development of Senegal through their involvement in the agricultural sector. Agriculture is the mainstay of the national economy and has long been the principal activity of the *shaykhs*. For over one hundred years they have been establishing villages where their *taalibés* cultivate groundnuts and various cereals in exchange for religious instruction. The number and size of the fields exploited by any one *shaykh*, and the resulting profits from the sale of produce, will largely depend on the number of *taalibés* willing to work for him. The Caliphs at the summit of the religious hierarchy are the custodians of literally thousands of hectares of agricultural land (villages like Touba-Bogo, Touba-Bélel, and Diaksao for example) and, given the cheapness of *taalibé* labor, control large revenues. On occasion they will even solicit the labor of *taalibés* of lesser *shaykhs*, in a system similar to the *corvée*. The *corvée* system is operational within a given brotherhood, but sometimes two brotherhoods will also cooperate in this way. The Tijānīs and Mourides of Salum for instance have been known to jointly cultivate fields belonging to one or the other. This exchange of service can be spread over time, allowing one *ṭarīqa* to "call in" its debt at a time most useful to it. It also serves as a practical way of improving relations between brotherhoods.

Another form of implication of the brotherhoods in agriculture are the collective fields cultivated on the behalf of *shaykhs* on land they do not necessarily control directly. *Taalibés* who work their own land will sometimes devote one day a week (often the Wednesday) during the growing season to cultivating a field for their *shaykh*. This is considered as compensation for the services they would be doing were they working directly for the *shaykh*. Theoretically, the *shaykh-murīd* relationship as understood by the masses of Senegalese adherents requires that the *murīd*, or *taalibé*, give himself over entirely to his *shaykh*'s will. This means physically devoting himself to satisfying the needs of his spiritual guide. This is impossible for *taalibés* who also have other obligations and who must earn a living far from their *shaykhs*. The Wednesday fields are material proof that the distant *taalibé* is not less devoted to his *shaykh* than the one who works in the *shaykh*'s own fields.

While the implication of the brotherhoods in agriculture has helped develop this crucial sector of Senegal's economy, it has come at a cost. The push to establish new villages, decade after decade, has meant the destruction of vast areas of forest and brush. In ecological terms, this caused an acceleration in the processes of desiccation and desertification which became acute in the 1970s. The *shaykhs* have been slow to understand the unsustainable nature of their agricultural activities but are now at last actively promoting reforestation campaigns. In many cases this is too little too late as the poverty of deteriorated soils has already led to mass rural exodus. The relative affluence of city life, or at least the promise of it, is a powerful pull factor and has contributed to this migration. Many *taalibés* come to the cities in search of work; some find it and some do not, some find seasonal employment and return periodically to their village, others become artisans, or traders. In most cases however the migration becomes permanent and they settle in the cities.

Rural-urban migration has modified the traditional *shaykh-murīd* relationship. At first, the urban *taalibés* of a *shaykh* would pool their resources and buy a field on the outskirts of town which they would farm collectively - like the Wednesday fields of their villages. In an urban context, this turned out not to be the most efficient solution to the problem of how to serve their *shaykh*. It is more usual now for urban *taalibés* to collect gifts in money or in kind which they will then present to their *shaykh*, or, increasingly, directly to the Caliph General himself. Each gives according to his or her means. The average worker might manage a donation of 500 or 1000 francs CFA per year. A civil servant will be able to give between 5000 and 10 000 francs CFA, while a successful merchant will give up to 50 000 or 100 000 francs CFA. Exceptionally, individual remittances of millions or even hundreds of millions of francs CFA have been made to the Caliph Generals. More than the revenues generated from agricultural production, the liquid assets constituted by these urban remittances have allowed the more enterprising *shaykhs* to improve their rural holdings, or expand into other sectors of the economy, like livestock, industry or commerce. In effect, dry farming in Senegal is severely limited by the short 3-month rainy season (July through September). Under these conditions, and in the absence of new virgin lands to exploit, it has become impossible to increase groundnut and cereal production. The *shaykhs* have now started to invest in irrigated lands and orchards, which produce fruit and vegetables all year round.

The more important *shaykhs* certainly command considerable resources, but they are also subject to many demands on the part of their *taalibés*. The Caliph-General especially is considered to be an inexhaustible source of funds, a veritable bank those in need will turn to, sometimes getting from him more than they put in. In practice, a good portion of whatever accumulates at the summit of the hierarchy circulates back down the echelons. First, every *shaykh*, from the Caliph-General on down, must feed and cloth the *taalibés* who live and work in his entourage. Secondly, *shaykhs* are obliged to see to the needs of the following categories of people:

1. *Poor members of their family or of the families of their* taalibés

If a brotherhood is managed as a private property, it is logical that poor relatives of those who manage it are the first to benefit from its resources. The Caliphs are surrounded and constantly solicited by a throng of destitute people requesting alms. Some of the destitute have physical handicaps, others are old, sick, or widowed. Many have spent their lives in the service of one or another *shaykh* and may still have children in their service.

2. *Poor Muslims who are not affiliated to the brotherhood*

Poverty can be considered as one of the factors which unite the various *ṭarīqas*. It destroys psychological barriers and entices the destitute party to seek help from all possible directions. Poor people regard any *shaykh*, of whatever stripe, as a person they can have recourse to in times of need. The *shaykh*, for his part, has the unconditional social and religious obligation to come to the aid of any Muslim requesting it. Sometimes the amount of aid, or more importantly the manner in which it is given, will entice the beneficiary to adhere to the donor *ṭarīqa*, as was the case with the poet Ibrāhīm Diop mentioned above. This poet had heavy debts and visited many *shaykhs* throughout the country requesting their help in paying them off. He was unlucky in his search until he met *Shaykh* Muḥammad Bamba Mbacké, who gave him exactly the sum needed. This apparently was enough to convince Ibrāhīm Diop to become a Mouride. The role of the *shaykh* as provider and sustainer is seen by the masses of adherents as related to his spiritual functions in the Hereafter. There is a local saying which goes: "He who cannot help you in this world will be unable to help you in the next"! What this means is that the more useful a *shaykh* is in socio-economic terms, the greater will be the hopes placed on his intercession on the Day of Judgment, and the more meritorious will be the act of giving him gifts and money. Alms-giving and charity are thus seen by donors as "investments" in the *ṭarīqa*. Some *shaykhs* skillfully exploit this sentiment by being seen always surrounded by poor alms-seekers. Wealthy donors are thus reassured - if reassurance is necessary - that their donations are being properly used for the needy, that the *shaykh* is simply an intermediary between the two social groups.

3. *The industrious and hard-working*

It sometimes happens that a wealthy *taalibé* finds himself in a precarious financial situation for one reason or another and seeks the help of his *shaykh*. Rather than giving the *taalibé* money from his own purse, the *shaykh* might intervene on his behalf with a bank, or with some other institution or individual affiliated with the *ṭarīqa*, to secure a loan. This loan is "guaranteed" by the *shaykh*. This form of internal solidarity among the various members and branches of the *ṭarīqa* is increasingly encouraged by the Caliphs. The brotherhoods as organizations are "umbrellas", beneath which many different types of businesses operate. Though cooperation among these businesses is increasing on the *ad hoc* basis just described, no real financial structure has yet been put in place.

The *ṭarīqa*'s "umbrella" can also, it is clear, be used to hide shady deals and to offer protection to business transaction of dubious legal, moral, and especially religious standing. Numerous fraud artists and smugglers have found sanctuary with some great *shaykh* and have thus kept out of reach of the long arm of the state's fiscal police. Easy money buys lots of friends. Since the early 1960s a number of Senegal's religious centers have become hubs for illicit trade and commerce as smugglers have set up shop in them. Goods bought in the Gambia were trucked across the border without customs duties being paid on them, and were then sold to Senegalese wholesalers at a hefty profit. This fraud involved not only household goods and appliances but also dangerous products like firearms and illegal drugs. The situation became so worrisome to the religious and the political authorities that clean-up campaigns had to be waged in order to rid these spiritual centers of the scoundrels who had found shelter in them. The highly publicized clean up of the religious cities did not however signify the end of fraud and rackets. This is because the brotherhoods are not the only Senegalese institutions to be infected by corruption. Traffickers and smugglers have forged links throughout the country and use a multiplicity of means to transport and exchange goods illegally. Real and/or false *shaykhs*, who market their high social status and connections, are but one among many fronts available to them. It is therefore unjust to single out the fraud committed under the mantle of the religious brotherhoods for special reprobation. Corruption is widespread in the Senegalese economy and society, and fraud is most often committed with the complicity of those whose duty it is to combat it. Fraud committed under the cover of the brotherhoods is no different in extent or content than the fraud which racks the rest of the country's economic activities. Unscrupulous men and women in pursuit of easy money can even use the good name of a *shaykh* without his knowledge or consent. Other *shaykhs* might lend themselves to this use. For instance, a smuggler who amasses a fortune and wants to preserve it is likely give a sizable portion of it to his *shaykh*. The smuggler will then understandably become very close to the *shaykh*, and associated to the *shaykh*'s activities. This tacit agreement will allow the *shaykh* to become more powerful and influential, and thus more able to protect his protégé. If the smuggler then encounters difficulties, the *shaykh* will mobilize all the material and moral means at his disposal to see him through the situation. If the *shaykh* were to fail in this, his prestige would diminish substantially. He would appear weak in the eyes of his *taalibés* and might loose some of them; no one wants to submit to a weak *shaykh*.

The economic activities of some senior members of the *ṭarīqas* are so vast that these *shaykhs* no longer devote time or energy to the fundamental and essential tasks of their brotherhoods. They have become businessmen in *shaykh*'s robes. They contribute the growth of the *ṭarīqas* in all the wrong ways, consolidating the brotherhoods as influential socio-economic networks but contributing nothing to education for instance. New disciples then flock to the brotherhoods for all the wrong reasons, in order to obtain favors and improve their situation in this world for instance. Ordinary people have come to measure the importance of a *shaykh* by the extent of his wealth and power and, in circular logic, rank the *ṭarīqas* according to the number of their adherents. The brotherhoods are admired and respected primarily for the material benefits they bring to the children of Adam. Spiritual benefits, apparently, come second.

The Brotherhoods and Social Life

Senegalese brotherhoods are influential in social life through the very same hierarchy of *shaykhs* and officials which regulates their spiritual functions. The social functions of the Caliph-General and his entourage of lieutenants often overshadow the spiritual ones. The masses of adherents see their Caliph and his *shaykhs* as a traditional chief and tribal council. Directives emanating from above, from the summit of the hierarchy, are closely followed by the rank-and-file. The speed with which decisions and initiatives from the top can be implemented reveals much about the influence these religious institutions wield within their communities.

The spiritual guidance of the *shaykh* is mostly manifest in the social and family life of his *taalibés*. For instance, it is often the *shaykh* who arranges the marriage of his *taalibé*. These marriages are usually contracted within the brotherhood and, not surprisingly, they serve to reinforce its internal structure of interlocking interests. Until recently, a *taalibé* who wanted to get married would first tell his *shaykh* of his intention and would indicate to him the identity of his desired bride. The *shaykh* would then send someone to see the father of the woman, or else would call the father to a meeting, and would inform him of his desire to see the daughter married to so-and-so, often unbeknownst to her. Such a request would be met with submissive acquiescence. The *shaykh* would set the date and place of the marriage celebration, the cost of which he would underwrite himself. It was the *shaykh*, on behalf of the groom, who would then transmit the dowry to the bride's family, but it was the groom's responsibility to make sure that the women of the bride's house were entirely satisfied with it.

This was a widely practiced system of betrothal, especially in rural Mouride communities, until recently. But it was not a very happy or successful one. Marriages contracted in this way often led to divorce and sore relations between the two families because the spouses did not know each other sufficiently prior to engagement. The submissive acquiescence of the bride's father was often insincere, and the bride herself was not even consulted. Religious leaders have now for the most part abandoned what was an unjust system. They will still arrange marriages, but these are now subject to discussion among all parties before engagements are made.

Likewise, serious disputes between spouses, or between their families, are often arbitrated by the *shaykh* or his representative. Generally speaking, the *shaykh*'s decisions are accepted by the men and rejected by women. This rejection on the part of women is not a sign of deliberate rebelliousness towards religious authority on their part. Rather, it reflects a persistent cultural condition in West Africa; women, more than men, continue to be influenced by local traditions which are not always compatible with Islamic precepts. However, the opposition of women to the decisions of *shaykhs* in marital and family disputes is a moot point. In most matters of family and social life, ultimate decisions are taken by men.

Beyond family matters, *shaykhs* are also responsible for resolving disputes between different factions within their brotherhood. This is especially the case, once again, in rural areas where people would much rather take their problems to the religious authorities than see them adjudicated in the courts of law. However, if the dispute involves members of two different *ṭarīqas*, its resolution through this parallel system can only occur if the *ṭarīqas* in question, or at least their local representatives, are on good terms. If not, then the parties will have no choice but to refer their case to the local judiciary. The *ṭarīqas* will then act as influential advocates, each intervening in support of its affiliate member. The success or failure of such intervention depends on the power and influence each is able to exercise.

Shaykhs intervene regularly with local public administrators and private entrepreneurs in order to secure jobs for their *taalibés*. There is a contradiction here in that the same brotherhoods who woefully neglect the education and training of their adherents nonetheless insist on seeing that they get the best jobs available. In any case, this aspect of the social involvement of the brotherhoods constitutes one of the most fertile fields in which to invest. By placing its members in key positions within state administration and its various organs, whether at the local, regional or national level, a brotherhood is able to multiply its influence. While serving the state, these civil servants will naturally also render service to their *ṭarīqa*.

A few years ago an association of Mouride civil servants was created. It disappeared shortly afterwards following a vitriolic attack against it by the satirical newspaper *Le Politicien*. The journal accused members of the association of opportunism and of seeking material benefit under the mantle of religion. The quiet disappearance of this association from the public eye does not however mean that it has ceased to exist. Mouride civil servants already have their own *dā'ira* (a "liaison agency" or "local bureau") which they first set up under *Shaykh* ᶜAbd al-Aḥad Mbacké, the third Caliph-General of the Mourides (1968-1989), with whom some of them maintained very close relations. *Shaykh* ᶜAbd al-Aḥad had also attempted to establish a permanent structure between the *dāʾira* of Mouride civil servants and that of Mouride students enrolled at the University of Dakar. The two agencies represented the greatest intellectual and financial aspirations of the *ṭarīqa.*

The *dāʾira* is a relatively recent phenomenon. It is an association of brothers who are in close contact with each other, either because of their jobs or because of their places of residence. For instance, a *dāʾira* might be set up by affiliates of a *ṭarīqa* who happen to work for the same company, or in the same factory, or government bureau. Sometimes it will be set up by the *taalibés* of a certain *shaykh* who happen to live in the same town. A *dāʾira,* as a local administrative organ of a *ṭarīqa*, usually has a President, a Vice-President, a Secretary-General and a Treasurer. It depends for its resources on the voluntary yearly contributions of its constituent members, and its role and activities will therefore reflect the number and affluence of these. *Dāʾiras* will meet once a week, or every month, to sensitize and spiritually mobilize its members, through collective recital of the panegyric poems of the *ṭarīqa*'s founder for instance. A *dāʾira* will organize, among other things, group visits to the residence of its spiritual guide, or to that of the Caliph-General in the *ṭarīqa*'s spiritual capital, where its members will remit the sums they have collected. Other funds are retained by the *dāʾira* to cover its operating expenses: radio announcements, bus rentals, etc.

Dāʾiras are truly administrative agencies. They play a crucial role in organizing the great festivals and commemorations which enliven Senegal's spiritual capitals on certain fixed dates each year. The two major sectarian events of the religious calendar are the Tijānī *Gamou* of Tivaouane,[90] and the Mouride *Magal* in Touba.[91] These ceremonies are supposed to commemorate beneficent events for which believers should show their gratitude to God by acts of sincere devotion. Hundreds of thousands of them will in fact flock to the sanctuaries in Touba, Tivaouane and elsewhere on these occasions. This travel constitutes a serious drain on the meager financial resources of most of the "pilgrims", with no apparent corresponding benefit to their spiritual progress. These events also occasion serious losses for Senegalese businesses and the public service, as employers and governmental agencies find themselves obliged to grant one or two days leave of absence to many employees.[92] Business in Dakar virtually comes to a halt at these times each year as the municipal buses are all chartered out for the transport of pilgrims. The citizens who remain behind cannot get to work. Those who gain most from these mass events are the local merchants and residents of the *ṭarīqa* centers. The merchants suddenly have a clientele of hundreds of thousands of out-of-towners and boost their stock accordingly, while local residents can purchase many items usually available only in the biggest cities.

Among the most active *dāʾiras* of young people is the Tijānī *Dāʾirat al-mustarshidīn wa'l-mustarshidāt*, administered by Muṣṭafā Sy, son of *Shaykh* Aḥmad Tidiane Sy. Thousands of young people of both sexes have joined it. It organizes a number of social and cultural activities which aim at promoting cooperation between its members and at strengthening their relation to their spiritual guide. Its weekly meetings are used to raise religious awareness. Its manifestly religious function has not however prevented this *dāʾira* from engaging in other kinds of activities. This is what worried the parent organization, the *zāwiya* of Tivaouane, whose members feared, rightly or wrongly, that the religious awareness of their children would be directed into non-religious pursuits. These worries were partially justified during the presidential and legislative elections of 1993, when the *Dāʾirat al-mustarshidīn wa'l-mustarshidāt* gave its unconditional support to the opposition *Parti Démocratique Sénégalaise*.

Such deviation from the objectives of the supreme authority of the *ṭarīqa*, whether real or apparent, can be fatal to a *dāʾira*, especially if the proper channels of authority are circumvented. This is what happened to the Mouride youth movement, the *Fédération des Jeunes Mourides*. The first cell of this federation was created in Dakar by a group of young Mourides who agreed on the necessity of combating the licentious behavior of many young people during Christmas and New Year's eve holidays. To counter the attractiveness of these un-Islamic festivities, they decided to organize Islamic ceremonies on these dates. After the success of their initial event, the group decided to expand the number and duration of subsequent activities. During a meeting held on 10 October 1980, the group decided to organize an "Islamic Cultural Week". A new administrative structure, called the "Commission for the Reorganization of the Union of Young Mourides of Senegal", was created to undertake the organization of the week-long festival. The new commission fixed the following objectives:

1.Create solidarity and encourage cooperation between Mourides,

2.Propagate the thought and the works of *Shaykh* Muḥammad Bamba Mbacké,

3.Promote religious instruction and training.

Henceforth, the federation held its annual meetings in Touba during the *Magal*. Reports presented during the annual general assembly held on Friday 1 November 1985 give an idea of the situation prevailing at the time:

- In 1984 there was in the city of Ziguinchor an umbrella association of six *dā'iras*. It wanted to expand but was facing difficulties due to the small number of Mourides in that city and to the fact they were mostly outsiders, there were few local people among them.
- In Diourbel there had been internal dissension among the representatives of the Federation and that city was therefore not represented at the general assembly.
- In Bambey an association of 11 *dā'iras* existed and was trying to rally others.
- In the city of Touba itself there were 18 *dā'iras* who had not joined the Federation, some of these had nonetheless sent observers to its general assembly.
- The Kaolack association had been very active since its creation in 1982. It had established a section in Nioro-du-Rip, while in the town of Fatick a group backed by the representative of the Caliph-General had been established on 10 January 1985.

- In Diacksao, in the same province, an association of 10 *dāʾiras* had been created in September 1985, but was encountering difficulties similar to those of Ziguinchor,
- In Tivaouane, the association created in 1984 was in serious financial trouble, with debts amounting to 150, 000 Francs CFA. Its President had been impeached as a result,
- The fledgling association in Saint-Louis was crippled by the lack of harmony among the *dāʾiras* of that city.

What this shows is the extent to which the Federation had succeeded in attracting young people. It had in effect become a social force of national scale and certain leaders of the political opposition were seeking to forge an alliance with it by offering to contribute much needed materiel to its social activities. During a major event organized at the Iba Mar Diop Stadium in Dakar in December 1986, the Federation's President warmly thanked the Secretary General of the *Parti Démocratique Sénégalais*, Abdoulaye Wade, for his material support.

This provoked a secret campain against the Federation, a campain for which agents were recruted who gave the Caliph-General of the Mourides detailed information about the activities undertaken by the Federation without his knowledge. At the same time they convinced him that enormous sums of money have been collected in the name of the *ṭarīqa* but had been used for personal purposes. This was sufficient to ignite the anger of *Shaykh* ᶜAbd Al-Aḥad. He took to national radio to denounce and disown the Federation, causing its immediate collapse. There can be little doubt that the Caliph-General's reaction in this instance had the effect of intimidating the leaders of Mouride *dāʾiras* and associations everywhere. Many simply withdrew from active social participation for fear of being accused in this way by political brokers and of arousing the displeasure of the Caliph.

The Brotherhoods and Politics

It should be clear by this point that given the variety and importance of their social and economic activities, the brotherhoods have acquired considerable political weight as well. The traditional political elite was the first to understand this. On three separate occasions in the last decades of the 19th century, dethroned local kings (*Damels* Lat Dior Diop and Samba Laobé Fall of Kayor, and *Bourba* Alboury Ndiaye of Jolof) contacted *Shaykh* Muḥammad Bamba Mbacké to propose an alliance; he would help them regain their lost crowns and they would defend Islam once back in power. The *shaykh* did not go along with these plans. He understood that the kings were not sincerely committed to Islam, that they simply wanted to use his religious authority for their purely political ends.

The colonial authorities were the next group to realize the political benefits that could be had by skillful use of the brotherhoods. Their basic policy was one of divide and rule. The colonial administration took full advantage of rivalries and enmities between the followers of the various *ṭarīqas*. They were set one against the other; in the administration's own words, "use their rivalries to subjugate then". Qādirī allies were recruited in Futa Toro to fight the Tijānīs and then Tijānī agents were recruited to spy on the Mourides. Prior to the rise of the Mourides as a spiritual and social force, the French colonizers had managed to win over a number of Qādirī and Tijānī *shaykhs* to their cause. In the 1860s the Qādirī *Shaykh* Bū Kunta of Ndiassane joined the camp of General Faidherbe and fought on his side against the army of *Damel* Macodou Fall of Kayor when the latter refused to abide by the 1858 truce with the French agreed to by his predecessor Birima Bambi Fall. *Shaykh* Bū Kunta also fought alongside the French in their final drive to occupy Kayor, in October 1886, when both Samba Laobé Fall and Lat Dior Diop were defeated and killed. According to Paul Marty, "Bū Kunta has demonstrated his loyalty by actively collaborating with us. He has marched with our forces on several occasions and has participated in military encounters. He has used his influence to quieten insurgent natives."[93] That is why the colonial administration addressed a letter of thanks to him dated 23 October 1886. We have seen above that *al-ḥājj* Mālik Sy, the spiritual guide of the largest contingent of Senegalese Tijānīs, though he did not go as far as *Shaykh* Bū Kunta in support of the colonial regime, did write a letter to the attention of his followers, dated 8 September 1912, requesting that they submit fully to the French and cooperate with them. During World War I *al-Ḥājj* Mālik Sy ordered his followers to pray for French victory and such prayers were offered in his *zāwiya* in Tivaouane.[94]

The colonial administration used certain *shaykhs* as intermediaries in their dealings with the subject masses and consequently these *shaykhs* acquired privileges. "Certainly the Qādiriyya and the Tijāniyya were not so much protected (by the colonial administration) as treated as honored prisoners. On the other hand, no leniency was shown towards the Sanūsīya, the Ahmadīya, the Mourides and the Hamallists."[95] The Mourides, as seen above, were repressed right from the start by the colonizers because the movement was seen by them as a continuation of the resistance of traditional political forces in new guise; many members of Senegal's deposed royalty had effectively rallied under the Mouride banner. Moreover, the Mouride *shaykhs*, beginning with Muḥammad Bamba, made no attempt to establish links with the colonial administration. As a social force, the Mouride movement was initially essentially a rural one. Its demographic base and its interests lay outside of the towns and cities where the colonial administration was most firmly in control. The distrust of Mourides towards the French turned to open hostility following the arrest and e1 1le of their leader and guide to Gabon. It was during the years of exile that the activities of certain Mouride *shaykhs* started to spread to the cities. They acquired property and found themselves obliged to adapt to urban life. They thus adopted a more conciliatory attitude towards the colonizers. This new approach permitted them to protect their urban interests and to convince the authorities to repatriate their exiled *shaykh*. We have already described the decisive roles played in this event by the wealthy Mouride *Shaykh* Ibra Fall and by the great Mauritanian ally of the French, *Shaykh* Sidiyya Bābā of Boutilimit.

Initially at least the overtly political role of the brotherhoods remained modest. Political life was limited to the registered citizens of the Four Communes (the municipalities of Gorée, Dakar, Rufisque and Saint-Louis), who alone had the right to vote. The rural masses and residents of other towns were politically irrelevant. The only *ṭarīqa* with a presence in the Four Communes was *al-ḥājj* Mālik Sy's Tijānī *zāwīya*. But *al-Ḥājj* Mālik Sy was not inclined to intervene in partisan politics in these municipalities, by telling his followers who to vote for, for instance. Perhaps he understood that an intervention of this type would be counter productive, as urban affiliates are not as blindly obedient to directives from their *shaykhs* as rural ones, especially in political matters. *Shaykh* Bū Kunta, on the other hand, had no qualms about intervening directly in elections. In the legislative elections of 1910 he ordered his followers to vote for a candidate who was also a close collaborator of his, serving him as lawyer and legal consultant. The *shaykh* obviously wanted to see his interested defended in the political realm as well. During the same period, other *shaykhs* were financing election campaigns, at the request of politicians who promised they would lend them their support and service their causes once elected. However, if the colonial authorities had hoped to turn the brotherhoods into docile tools of their administration, they were frustrated so long as the founding *shaykhs* were at the helm. Neither *al-ḥājj* Mālik Sy nor Muḥammad Bamba Mbacké, nor even their senior disciples were interested in this kind of a relationship with the political authorities. With time however a new generation of *shaykhs* emerged within the brotherhoods, and the colonial authorities approached these younger men. As the founding figures grew older and physically weaker, and were no longer in day to day control of their organizations, the younger *shaykhs* began to jostle for position. The political authorities took a keen interest in this development, and it is especially the thorny question of succession to the Caliphate of the brotherhoods that furnished them with the lever they needed to exercise influence over these religious institutions.

Al-ḥājj Mālik Sy wanted to designate Saydou Nourou Tall, grandson of *al-Ḥājj* ᶜUmar Tall, as successor to leadership of the *zāwīya* of Tivaouane, but Saydou Nourou Tall declined the offer, wanting to maintain his Caliphate over his grandfather's followers as a distinct Tijānī entity. As a result, it is *al-Ḥājj* Mālik Sy's eldest son, Abū Bakr, who became Caliph in 1922. Dissensions between the new Caliph and his brothers soon came to the fore and politicians exploited these. Abū Bakr Sy undoubtedly had political acumen and the authorities saw in him an intelligent long-term ally. In the end, he was only able to consolidate his leadership position through the support of the colonial authorities. Tensions within the Tijānī *zāwīya* in Tivaouane nonetheless continued to fester below the surface. Trust between the brothers was all but ruined and the Caliph eventually accused his younger siblings of wanting to depose him.

The problem then became acutely political. Following World War II political franchise was progressively widened beyond the Four Communes. Ever greater numbers of Senegalese subjects acquired the right to vote and the massive demographic base of the brotherhoods became the favorite target of politicians. When, during the June 1951 elections for the French National Assembly, the Socialist Party (SFIO) under Lamine Guèye organized a rally in Tivaouane, its partisans were met by the Caliph's followers with a hail of stones. A street battle resulting in deaths, injuries and material damages followed, and the SFIO failed to take the Tivaouane seat.[96] Though neither the Caliph nor his brothers had taken any partisan position in public, the Caliph's son, *Shaykh* Tidiane Sy was a staunch supporter of Léopold Senghor's *Bloc Démocratiqu*, and as a consequence Tijānī followers drew their own conclusions as to the political affiliation of their *shaykhs*. Dissension between the Sy brothers was to become very public during the *Gamou*[97] that December, when two of the Caliph's brothers, Manṣūr and ᶜAbd al-ᶜAzīz, refused to preside over the ceremony at his side. An emergency meeting of the most important Tijānī *shaykhs* was called to try to resolve the dispute and reunite the Sy family, but to no avail. Political interests and the fanaticism of a handfull of *taalibés* conspired to divide the *zāwīya* further. During the 1956 municipal election campaign, followers of the Caliph and those of his brother Mansour Sy came to blows, causing deaths, serious injury and a great conflagration in the city, followed by arrests and trials before the courts.[98] The following year witnessed the death first of Caliph Abū Bakr Sy and then, within days, of his brother and most likely successor Mansour Sy. The third brother, *al-Ḥājj* ᶜAbd al-ᶜAzīz Sy, has occupied the position of Caliph ever since. At the beginning of his Caliphate, ᶜAbd al-ᶜAzīz Sy had to face the opposition of his nephew, *Shaykh* Tidiane Sy, but the majority of his predecessor's followers nonetheless recognized the authority of the new Caliph. Stability, harmony and cohesion were eventually reestablished in Tivaouane. ᶜAbd al-ᶜAzīz Sy's noble character and many qualities are without a doubt the principal reasons the *zāwīya* founded by his father is still the prestigious, respected institution it is today.

The Mouride brotherhood in Touba also experienced succession disputes similar to those of Tivaouane. *Shaykh* Muḥammad Bamba died in 1927 without designating a successor. His brother, *Shaykh* Anta Mbacké considered himself to be the legitimate successor and found support in Muḥammad al-Fadil (also known as Serigne Falilou), Muḥammad Bamba's second son. However, Muḥammad Bamba's eldest surviving brother, *Shaykh* Ibrāhīm Mbacké (also known as Mame Tierno) believed that the position should go to the founder's eldest son, Muḥammad al-Muṣṭafā Mbacké. The entire Mouride leadership, like the Mbacké family, was divided on the issue, though the majority of the disciples of the deceased founder recognized Muḥammad al-Muṣṭafā. The colonial authorities, convinced that the young Muḥammad al-Muṣṭafā would be more willing to collaborate with them than his wealthy uncle *Shaykh* Anta, supported his candidacy and intervened directly to resolve the dispute in his favor. M. Brévié, the Director of Political Affairs for the Colony of Senegal, traveled personally to Touba to lecture the antagonists there. He made it clear to the assembly that those who did not submit to the authority of Muḥammad al-Muṣṭafā Mbacké would incurr the displeasure of the colonial administration. Understandably, this direct intervention and threat of sanctions on the part of the colonizers angered the venerable *shaykhs* of the older generation, to the point where the very pious and usually reserved *Shaykh* Mbacké Bousso wrote a letter to the authorities protesting their interference in the internal affairs of the *ṭarīqa*. He explained that the disciples and followers of *Shaykh* Muḥammad Bamba had not joined him for reasons of material benefit, that his passing had not altered their situation and that they knew better than anyone else what their duties towards Muḥammad al-Muṣṭafā were.

In any case, in order to assert his authority over his father's legacy, Muḥammad al-Muṣṭafā Mbacké did not only rely on the colonial administration, he also had powerful political friends. In effect, he had made an alliance with Blaise Diagne, the first Senegalese representative to sit in the National Assembly in Paris, where he represented the Four Communes from 1914 to 1934. Muḥammad al-Muṣṭafā's rival for supremacy over the Mourides, *Shaykh* Anta Mbacké, gave his full backing to Blaise Diagne's rival on the political scene, Ngalandou Diouf, who represented the commune of Rufisque in the Colonial Council and whom the colonial authorities despised and feared for his anti-racist stance. In 1930 *Shaykh* Anta Mbacké was arrested and el lled to the French Sudan (Mali) for his continued opposition to the Caliphate of his nephew. In 1934 however, Blaise Diagne died and was succeeded as deputy for Senegal by Ngalandou Diouf, who managed to have *Shaykh* Anta Mbacké released from prison and repatriated.

The main area of leverage of the colonial administration over Muḥammad al-Muṣṭafā Mbacké was the construction of Touba's great mosque. The Caliph of the Mourides saw it as his principle task to complete the mosque which his father had long wanted to build and had actually started in the last year of his life. In order to complete the mosque, the Caliph would need to muster all the resources at his disposal, and others as well that only the colonial administration could provide. This administration had already given authorization for construction to *Shaykh* Muḥammad Bamba. Following his death the colonial administration created a legal problem over the transfer of authorization, which forced Muḥammad al-Muṣṭafā to have recourse to it in search of a resolution. With the new Caliph firmly in power and in their political debt, the colonial authorities contributed in material ways to the construction of Touba's great mosque.

In 1945 a second succession dispute rocked the Mouride brotherhood, and once more the colonial authorities played a key role in its resolution. When Muḥammad al-Muṣṭafā died, his eldest son, *Shaykh* AḥmadMbacké, considered himself to be the legitimate successor but the majority of Mouride *shaykhs*, including nearly all the senior members of the Mbacké family, chose his uncle and Muḥammad Bamba's eldest surviving son, Muḥammad al-Fāḍil, as Caliph. Though the colonial authorities immediately recognized Muḥammad al-Fāḍil as Caliph of the

Mourides, his nephew and rival decided to push his claim any way. *Shaykh* AḥmadMbacké took possession of the deeds and titles to Touba's great mosque, which the colonial administration had so cleverly established in his father's name following the first succession dispute, and which as principal legatee he believed he had rights to. Construction of the mosque had been suspended during World War II and could not be resumed until the matter of authority over the site was again resolved. With the help of the colonial administration, Muḥammad al-Fadil had the entire site of Touba including its mosque designated as collective property belonging to all the descendants of the founder jointly. And with his new title of Caliph-General, he had ultimate and undisputed authority over the whole enterprise.

Like Tivaouane, Touba became a political battle ground in this period. In the French legislative elections of June 1951, Léopold Senghor's "Bloc Démocratique" obtained the official backing of the Mouride Caliph-General, while Lamine Guèye's SFIO was supported by *Shaykh* Aḥmad Mbacké. The SFIO was trounced. The scenario was repeated again the following year in elections for representation in the Territorial Assembly. The uncle and the nephew again publicly endorsed the competing parties and violent clashes between opposing militants ensued in Touba itself, resulting in casualties and culminating in an attack on the Caliph's own residence. In 1958, after repeated electoral defeats, the SFIO quietly merged with Senghor's Bloc Démocratique and a reconciliation of sorts occurred within the Mbacké family. *Shaykh* Aḥmad Mbacké nonetheless remained a formidable opposition figure within the Mouride community until his death in 1978. Muḥammad al-Fāḍil, Caliph-General of the Mourides, remained, for his part, one of President Senghor's staunchest allies until his death in 1968.

Though he was not Muslim, in the decade leading up to independence in 1960 President Léopold S. Senghor succeeded in obtaining the support of Muḥammad al-Fāḍil and other leading *shaykhs* against his main political rival, Lamine Guèye (d. 1968), who was Muslim. This success was partly due to his competence as a politician, his professional and courteous treatment of friend and foe alike, and his ability to give the *shaykhs* what they wanted.

Some *shaykhs* however were opposed to his policies. At various times Ibrāhīm Niasse of Kaolack, *Shaykh* Aḥmad Mbacké, eldest son of the first Caliph of the Mourides, and ᶜAbd al-Aḥad Mbacké, the third Mouride Caliph-General, all openly expressed criticism of his policies. They were mainly concerned with the President's ability to divide Senegal's *shaykhs* against each other, a situation they saw as being detrimental to Islam. President Senghor, in effect inherited the policy of "divide and rule" from the colonial administration he supplanted, and in the process he initiated a new "Muslim policy" for Senegal.

Indeed, it was Senghor who caused the collapse of the *Conseil Supérieur Islamique*, the first and last unified political organ Senegal's *shaykhs* ever created. The Council was set up by the leaders of the most important brotherhoods in 1958 and represented the aspirations of many Muslims. It had three objectives:

1. To control the drafting of a constitution for Senegal and to make sure no constitution would be implemented without its approval.
2. To act as mediator in disputes between the State and the Muslim community, or its spiritual leaders.
3. To defend the interests of Muslims.

The Council consisted of the following members:

- Seydou Nourou Tall, President (Tijāniyya)
- Muḥammad al-Fāḍil Mbacké, President (Mouride)
- Muḥammad al-Bashīr Mbacké, Vice-President (Mouride)
- Ibrāhīm Niasse, Secretary (Tijāniyya)
- *Shaykh* Aḥmad Mbacké, Secretary (Mouride)
- ᶜAbd al-ᶜAzīz Sy, Treasurer (Tijāniyya)
- Muḥammad Awa Balla Mbacké, Assistant-Treasurer (Mouride)

The very first request of the Council was that Muslims be guaranteed 40 of the 80 seats in the proposed Legislative Assembly. This was certainly a modest demand but was symptomatic of a political consciousness among the brotherhood leadership which, if allowed to develop, would have lent support to the opposition politicians who moved in their circle. Senghor, an extremely intelligent politician, fully appreciated this eventuality. His first response to the Council's demand was that it was too modest! The 40 Muslim seats proposed were not enough for a country where the great majority of citizens are Muslim. He proposed to increase this number substantially, but under the condition that those who would occupy the seats in the Legislature be independent of the Council. In other words, they would have to be Muslims but would not have to represent or defend the views of the "Islamic Supreme Council". Secondly, Senghor refused to deal with the Council as an institution, preferring to negotiate with individual *shaykhs* separately. He came to agreements with them on this basis whereby he would provide them with funds. In this way he hamstrung the Council without having to officially dissolve it.

The alliance between certain powerful *shaykhs* and Senghor—despite his famous claim that if he could not turn Muslims away from their religion he could at least turn them into bad Muslims—was one of the greatest paradoxes in the contemporary political history of Senegal. President Senghor was surrounded by Muslims who were entirely devoted to his policies and who served as intermediaries with the *shaykhs*. These intermediaries became so close to the *shaykhs* that a situation came to pass when nothing was withheld from them any more. Senghor, being so well informed of the internal affairs of the brotherhoods and their leaders, was able to implement decisions even when these were contrary to the teachings of Islam, the basis of the spiritual authority of the *shaykhs*. By 1962 Senghor was in full control. He no longer worried about opposition on the part of the *shaykhs*; in all cases this opposition, though sometimes vehement, would be short lived. He was thus able to implement policies even if the *shaykhs* considered them to be un-Islamic. He was able to rapidly crush their opposition without having to make any concessions of his own.

The best example of Senghor's skillful management of the *shaykhs* was the 1972 bill on Family Law. When the President consulted the *shaykhs* about the proposed legislation, they unanimously rejected those parts they considered to be contrary to the *sharīᶜa* and published a 17 page declaration (dated 3 January

1972) explaining their view. Not withstanding this, the Senegalese National Assembly passed the bill and it became law (bill n° 72-61, 12 June 1972)[99] Since then, the relationship between the *shaykhs* and the political authorities have been marked by the greatest of contradictions. The majority of the brotherhood leaders have consistently given their unflinching support to the governing party irrespective of its attitudes and policies towards Islam. And they have done this with the sole purpose of protecting their vested interests.

The Mouride *shaykhs* are often accused of being the chief culprits of this paradoxical situation. Without a doubt, of all the *ṭarīqas*, the Mourides carry the most political weight. They are a major economic institution and rank-and-file Mourides are generally more submissive to the political directives of their spiritual guides than those other brotherhoods. An important fraction of the Mouride leadership not only refuse to use their prestige and influence in support of the Muslim community, they loudly proclaim their support for the governing party with little apparent benefit to themselves or to Islam. In truth this has not always been the case. There have been times when the relations between the Mouride *ṭarīqa* and the political authorities have been quite cool. This was most notable during the first years of the Caliphate of *Shaykh* ᶜAbd al-Aḥad Mbacké, in the late 1960s and early 1970s. For both political and religious reasons, ᶜAbd al-Aḥad Mbacké had never been sympathetic to President Senghor. For 12 uneasy years relations between the government and the *ṭarīqa* remained strained and President Senghor never managed to befriend the third Caliph-General of the Mourides as he had his predecessor. He nonetheless managed to achieve his objectives through other channels.

When Abdou Diouf, a Muslim, succeeded Senghor to the Presidency in 1981 he immediately established excellent relations with Caliphs of Senegal's various brotherhoods, and with *Shaykh* ᶜAbd al-Aḥad Mbacké in particular. In fact the Caliph-General of the Mourides became the principal political ally of the new President and committed himself and his institution to him in a manner unprecedented in the history of Senegal's Islamic brotherhoods. This commitment can be explained in part by the generous patronage the government has bestowed on the city of Touba, the "capital" of the Mourides, but mostly by the great material and financial contributions of the government to the Caliph's various projects. Moreover, the President designated *Shaykh* ᶜAbd al-Aḥad his "favored councilor" and, it was rumored, would decide nothing of importance without consulting with the Caliph-General first. It was believed, especially by Mourides, that the opinions of the Caliph-General were considered with the highest regard by the political authorities. In fact, it is apparent that the government's decisions and policies bore little resemblance to those opinions which the Caliph-General expressed publicly. It seems that ᶜAbd al-Aḥad Mbacké was content simply with the status of most favored councilor. He was the only national religious leader to receive regular visits (every three months) from the President, who styled himself "Father of the Nation" and who was known to have addressed the Mouride Caliph as "my father"!

Many Muslims were surprised and others shocked when ᶜAbd al-Aḥad Mbacké seemed to put the entire *ṭarīqa* in jeopardy by publicly endorsing the incumbent candidate during the February 1988 Presidential elections. In his usual tone he declared that "whoever does not vote for Abdou Diouf in the elections has betrayed Muḥammad Bamba."[100] This meant in concrete terms that any Mouride *taalibé* who voted for another candidate was effectively excluding him/herself from the *ṭarīqa*. This unusual directive from above deeply troubled many Mourides who were politically engaged in opposition parties, and especially with the principal one, the *Parti Démocratique Sénégalaise* (PDS). An unprecedented rift emerged within the Mouride community as a result. Most of the rural *taalibés* obeyed their *shaykh*'s directive and voted for Abdou Diouf. Another fraction of Mourides preferred to abstain from casting a ballot in order to maintain a clear conscience. Yet a third fraction, comprising mostly urban Mourides, voted for opposition candidates despite the directive. In justifying their decision, these *taalibés* declared that their Sufi engagement was of a religious nature and not a political one, and that the founder of the *ṭarīqa*, Muḥammad Bamba, had not recommended a specific political orientation to his disciples nor had he ever asked them to support a politician or a political party.

Shaykh ᶜAbd al-Aḥad Mbacké was severely attacked in the press, as no previous Caliph had ever been, for being self-serving and power-hungry. Furthermore, at a moment of massive popular unrest, the political opposition held him directly responsible for disrupting the electoral process. Moreover, the Caliph-General does not seem to have enjoyed any obvious benefits in return for his overt support of the President's candidacy, in any case no more so than other *shaykhs* who provided only implicit support or who chose to remain neutral. On the contrary, the Mouride brotherhood emerged from the ordeal manifestly weaker than it have ever been. For the very first time its spiritual guide had been the object of personal attack by the press and by opposition politicians, despite the respect and prestige inherent in the position. This negative outcome did not come as a surprise to political observers in Senegal. The Mouride brotherhood has often been freely exploited. The political authorities have always been able to commandeer it for their purposes and, despite appearances to the contrary, the brotherhood has never gained any special political influence on decision making in return.

A now standard assessment of Senegal's political landscape, which stems from the analysis of Paul Marty early in the century, considers the Tijāniyya *ṭarīqa* as representing normative Islam. The key State-controlled religious functions have traditionally been exercised by Tijānīs: the Imamate of Dakar's Great Mosque (even though the Mourides made the largest financial contribution during its construction).[101] the *Ḥajj* Commissioner is very often a Tijānī figure, and official Senegalese representation to the major international Islamic institutions are also usually Tijānīs. According to this same assessment, the Mourides are a local phenomenon and can be used for immediate political purposes at minimal cost. Generally speaking, Tijānī *shaykhs* have shown a more finely tuned political acumen than their Mouride counterparts. This helps to explain the relatively privileged stature of their brotherhood vis-à-vis the State.

This is best illustrated by the career of *Shaykh* Tidiane Sy. Contrary to other *shaykhs*, *Shaykh* Tidiane Sy is an experienced politician who plays the field with foresight according to astute calculations. He is extremely intelligent and audacious and knows all the hidden undercurrents of Senegalese politics. His silence and his voiced opinion alike are priceless. With some justification, he has assessed his own value thus: "Some are paid to speak but I am paid to keep quiet". In 1987, in the lead up to the aforementioned Presidential elections, and after a long political career, *Shaykh* Tidiane Sy created the "Movement for the Reelection of President Abdou Diouf". Following the President's electoral victory however, the relations between the two politicians deteriorated.

The political situation in Senegal has evolved since 1988. ᶜAbd al-Aḥad Mbacké, Caliph-General of the Mourides and chief ally of President Diouf, died in June 1989. His successor, *Shaykh* ᶜAbd al-Qādir Mbacké was far too old for the political game. His attitude with regard to power can be summed up by the Arabic term "*mudārah*", which means careful attention, or consideration.[102] Some pressure was put on him to adopt the attitude of his predecessor but this quite obviously went against his world view. In any case *Shaykh* ᶜAbd al-Qādir was only Caliph-General for a brief period before his death in May 1990. The fifth Caliph-General of the Mourides, *Shaykh* Ṣāliḥ Mbacké, is intelligent, well-informed and advocates neutrality in all political matters. He maintains this position despite the fact that the State has granted him 45,000 hectares of virgin land for Mouride agricultural exploitation.

Politicians now have a free reign to recruit allies among those *shaykhs* they believe still control votes. In the Presidential elections of February 1993, and again in the Legislative elections of May of the same year, each political party in fact obtained the support of one or several *shaykhs*. Mouride and Tijānī *shaykhs* vied with each other in their support of various candidates, with the incumbent President Diouf and his party winning most favors. Serigne ᶜAbd al-ᶜAzīz Sy Jr. and Serigne Modou Bousso Dieng Mbacké were particularly conspicuous in their support for Diouf, whereas some of their brothers, nephews and cousins went all out in support of opposition candidates. Some, like Muṣṭafā Sy, went too far in their political involvement.[103] *Shaykhs* who enter the political fray in a cavalier fashion, without having thought their involvement through, end up by disrupting the democratic process. To stop citizens from voting for the candidate of their choice goes against all the rules of democracy. The immediate consequence of such an act is that the injured parties become hostile to Islam and hold it responsible for the actions of its irresponsible representatives. In fact, Islam itself has not benefited at all from the political involvement of its supposed representatives. On the contrary, the mockery of Islamic symbols in theater and cinema, the censorship of serious Islamic debate, the encroaching secularization of family law, the exclusion of religious education from public schooling, all indicate that the State has taken no account of the views and opinions of Senegal's religious leaders.

CHAPTER EIGHT

THE FUTURE OF THE BROTHERHOODS IN SENEGAL

The history of religions follows a fixed path set according to a divine law qualified by the Qurān as unalterable. Emergent religious systems like Sufism possess an internal dynamic which propels them forward regardless of whether or not they conform to the theoretical foundations of the religions from which they spring. Later, they begin to loose this dynamism and progressively cease to expand until a new force emerges to propel them forward again...or replace them. The Sufi brotherhoods of Senegal cannot escape from this unalterable pattern. The African founders and propagators of the brotherhoods were convinced that these religious institutions were the most efficient means of bringing people to Islam. Within a few years they effectively managed to attract massive adherence. Yet the majority of new proselytes did not gain a sound understanding of the underlying principles of the *ṭarīqa* and were thus unable to conform to its requirements in practice. The masses of followers adopted a sentimental attachment, which often verged on fanaticism, to the institutional structure itself. The brotherhoods of Senegal have thus evolved into something similar to local religious cults where rivalries have replaced cooperation and mutual solidarity.

For the past century or so, the brotherhoods have been characterized by two contrary phenomena. The fate of these institutions in the future could well be determined by the definitive victory of one tendency over the other. The first phenomenon is represented by the objectives of the founding *shaykhs*, who strove to establish firm fraternal relations between all Muslims. They gave priority to the building and strengthening of fraternity among believers and worked towards this objective wherever possible. The second phenomenon is represented by the tendency of the masses within each brotherhood to place added value on its supposed specificity and superiority over the others. This tendency leads them to identify themselves with the *ṭarīqa* and to use their *ṭarīqa* affiliation as a source of pride, prestige and privilege. In order to justify their claim to distinction, they will latch on to insignificant traditions relating to their founding *shaykh*, yet they will show no such punctilious enthusiasm when it comes to understanding and applying the fundamental teachings of this same *shaykh*. This attitude stems from the inability of rank-and-file followers to reconcile the teachings of the *shaykhs* which clearly state that all *ṭarīqas* are equally valid to the extent that they can all allow the believer to obtain God's pleasure, and the *shaykhs'* claims that their own specific *ṭarīqa* is the best one and the most apt to fulfill belief. The following verses from *Shaykh* Muḥammad Bamba Mbacké's *Masālik al-Jinān* illustrate the first proposal:

> Every *wird* leads the postulant
> To divine presence without detour,
> Whether it stems from al-Jīlānī,
> Or from Aḥmad al-Tijānī,
> Or from some other one of the poles,
> For they are all on the straight path.

There are few today, it must be noted, who can reconcile the notion of equality of the Sufi paths and the contrary notion of the superiority of one path over others - as both notions emanate from the *shaykhs* themselves. The uneducated *taalibés*, and they are in the majority, will end up by adopting the attitude most compatible with their sentimental sectarian attachments and may even succeed in imposing their view in this matter on their spiritual guides, who know better. The greater are the material interests of the *shaykhs*, the greater is the likelihood that they will espouse the sectarian view rather than the concept of universal Islamic fraternity. The brotherhoods today are run by men who have many such vested interests and tomorrow, given the policy of an inherited Caliphate, may well be led by men who no longer even feel the need to camouflage these interests. One can be permitted to predict that leaders such as these will be pawns in the hands of the masses of *taalibés*. They will take decisions based on their need to please their followers and to maintain their economic and social influence in the country.

The brotherhoods of Senegal have thus reached the inevitable point of exhaustion. Their initial force no longer propels them and they have become mired by the dead weight of ignorant masses. This explains why those voices who call for a return to normative Islamic practice based on universally recognized principles have trouble making themselves heard. They emanate from a small minority of educated *taalibés*. They usually get a cool reception from their *shaykhs* and are treated with genuine hostility by the masses of their brothers. They are considered to be a threat to the popular basis of the brotherhoods, which are founded on the belief in the capacity of the *shaykh* to lead his *taalibés* to Paradise by the easiest possible route, regardless of their conduct in this life, so long as they submit to and serve him with complete and utter devotion. If the Caliphs were to welcome and support this enlightened and reform-minded fraction of their followers and make use of their intellectual resources they would be able to rid the brotherhoods of the corrupt elements who exploit them to further purely material interests. This would certainly alienate the mass of followers and would reduce considerably the social, economic and political influence of the brotherhoods. The "popularity" of these religious institutions would suffer as a consequence and this would have far-reaching consequences for Senegal. The salvation of the brotherhoods as Islamic institutions however must come at this price. Maintenance of the status quo, on the other hand, is a recipe for slow death.

There is now a new, more critical awareness of the requirements of belief growing among Senegalese Muslims. This has much to do with the proliferation of the aforementioned modern Islamic schools in all regions of the country, the increasing contact between rural areas and cities due to rural exodus, the intense inter-personal networks characteristic of African traditions and Islamic societies both, and the increasing diffusion of mass media. People will no longer blithely accept what they are told. Directives from *shaykhs* are now open to question, especially if their conformity with the Qur'ān and the *Sunna* is not at first evident.

Mentalities and attitudes have definitely changed. There is more contact between Senegal and other parts of the Muslim world. Ever increasing numbers of Senegalese are literate in Arabic and are active in Islamic cultural and social organizations not affiliated to the *ṭarīqas* and whose common aim is the rational propagation of Islam. Their rules of order are clearly understood by all and their leaders are freely elected on the basis of their intellectual and moral merits. There is a consensus among these non-brotherhood associations that priority must be given to modern Islamic education. They have acquired a large audience in Senegal mostly because of the success of their various projects which serve as visible proof of the relevance of their methods. It is not likely that these socio-cultural associations will replace the brotherhoods in the near future. They can however serve as the much needed agents of reform for Islam in Senegal, in as much as they transcend Sufi affiliation and are able to bring together individuals with the required skills and abilities.

CHAPTER NINE

CONCLUSION

Sufism has long existed in Islam, as it is based on renunciation (*zuhd*) of superfluous concerns, an attitude advocated by both the Qur'ān and the *Sunna*. A rather specific and narrow understanding of this founding principle led to its application in real life and to the emergence of a distinct group of believers characterized by their austerity and abnegation in all matters relating to food, clothing and sexual relations. An entire system of values was then created on the basis of this austere behavior, and this is what has been known since the second century AH as *taṣawwuf*. *Taṣawwuf* evolved through several stages before taking the form of popular religious brotherhoods know as *ṭarīqas*. These popular religious institutions played a decisive part in spreading Islam among the African masses. The most well known in Senegal are the Qādiriyya, the Tijāniyya and the Murīdiyya. It has become apparent while describing the history and activities of these various *ṭarīqas* that they are inextricably linked to the country's recent history and to its cultural and social conditions, and that they have had a great impact on its population. Until quite recently the average Senegalese citizen was incapable of conceiving Islam outside of a Sufi affiliation.

Following an initial phase of intense religious activity under the leadership of the founders,, Senegal's brotherhoods entered a phase of stagnation. The *shaykhs* who succeeded the founders were more concerned with the management of inherited material interests than in the spiritual education and guidance of the masses of followers. As material prosperity has grown, spiritual fulfillment has diminished. Senegal's *shaykhs* today bear a closer resemblance to traditional West African chiefs than to the austere and dedicated Islamic educators their fathers were. The great mass of followers are content with this situation as they benefit materially from it. Only a small fraction of enlightened *taalibés* are demanding a return to the original educational mission. These reformers are nonetheless resolved to pursue their action and are increasingly successful in convincing their fellow Muslims to give material and moral support to their cause. Just as painful surgery is sometimes essential to saving a life, so too do they believe that reform of the brotherhoods is imperative to their survival as Islamic institutions. The success of this reform will determine the destiny of Islam in Senegal and its capacity to contribute to the development of the country in the future.

NOTES FROM CHAPTERS

N.B. No notes in Chapter 8 or in 9: "Conclusion."

FOREWORD AND INTRODUCTION

1 Census of Population, temporary results, published in 1988. According to this source, Muslims constitute 94% of the population and nearly 95% of them claim affiliation to a religious brotherhood.

2 Aḥmad ᶜIyāḍ, *Al-Taṣawwuf al-Islâmî*, Cairo, 1970, p. 62.

CHAPTER 1

3 Ibn al-Jawzî, *Talbîs Iblîs*, Beirut, n.d., pp. 154-155.

4 Aḥmad Iyāḍ, *Al-Tasawwuf al-Islâmî*, pp. 109-110, citing *Al-Munqidh min al-Ḍalâl* (Cairo, 1970).

5 Ibn Taymiyya, *Al-Fatāwā* (Riyadh, 1981), vol. 11, p. 18.

6a Aḥmad ᶜIyāḍ, *Al-Taṣawwuf al-Islâmî*, Cairo, 1970, p. 49.

6b Ibn al-ᶜArabī's full name is: Muḥyī 'l-Dīn Abū ᶜAbd Allāh Muḥammad b. ᶜAlī b. Muḥammad b. al-ᶜArabī al-Ḥātimī al-Ṭā'ī, known as Shaykh al-Akbar See *EI* (2), iii, 707, where it states: "He is usually referred to—incorrectly— as Ibn ᶜArabī, without the article, to distinguish him from Ibn al-ᶜArabī, Abū Bakr; in Turkey he is often referred to as "Muḥyī 'l-Dīn ᶜArabī" .

CHAPTER 2

7 al-Suhrawardi, *ᶜAwārif al-Maᶜārif*, marginal notes in Al-Ghazālī's *Ihyā' ᶜulūm al-dīn* , Cairo, 1957, vol. 4, p. 132.

8 Al-ᶜAsqalānī, *Sharḥ Ṣaḥîh, al-Bukhârî* Ryadh, n.d., vol. 12, p. 384.

9. Aḥmad ᶜIyāḍ, *Al-Taṣawwuf al-Islāmī*, Cairo, 1970, pp. 280-282.

CHAPTER 3

10 The most common Qâdîrî *dhikr* , which every disciple must recite after each statutory prayer, goes as follows:

> "God suffices us; what an excellent protector" 200 times,
> "I beg forgiveness from God, the Immense..." 200 times,
> "There is no god but God, the King, the Real, the Evident" 100 times,
> The *Prayer for the Prophet*, 100 times.

11. Ayyad, *Al-Taṣawwuf al-Islāmī*, Cairo, 1970.

12 *Ibid*, 282.

13 See Moustapha Ndiaye, "Rapport entre Qâdirites et Tijânites au Futa Toro aux XIX*e* et XX*e* siècles à travers *Al-Ḥaqq al-mubīn* de Cheikh Moussa Kamara,,"in *Bulletin de l'IFAN*, vol. 41, no. i, 1979, pp. 190 ff.

14 P. Marty, *Etudes sur l'Islam au Sénégal*, Paris, 1917, vol. 1, p. 204.

15 P. Marty, *op. cit.*, vol. 1, p. 35.

16 Aidara, *Qiṣsat Dar al-Khayr* , MS Dakar, IFAN, Ziguinchor, 514, p. 49, unpublished.

17 *Le Soleil*, April 20, 1988.

CHAPTER 4

18 ᶜAli Ḥarāzim, *Jawâhir al-Maᶜānî,* vol. 1, p. 32, Cairo, 1927.

19 *Ibid.*

20 This careful political planning on the part of its founder could not prevent the Tijāniyya *tarīqa* from being racked by internal succession disputes over the caliphate as the 19*t*h century progressed.

21 *Ibid.*, I, p. 43.

22 The *shahāda*, or "witnessing," is the first of the five canonical pillars of Islam and consists in testifying: "There is no god but God, and Muḥammad is the Messenger of God."

23 A famous quarrel about the number of times to recite the *Jawharat al-Kamāl* rocked the Tijânîya *tarîqa* in the 1930's. The "Hamālliyya" faction of the *tarîqa* maintained the original number of recitations at 11, while the majority of Tijânî *shaykhs* believed that this number had been abrogated and that the prayer should be recited 12 times. We shall not discuss the Hamālliyya Tijânîs here, as they do not have much of following in Senegal.

24 *Ibid.*, vol. 1, p. 111-112.

25 *Ibid.*, vol. 1, p. 136-187.

26 *Al-ḥājj* ᶜUmar Tall, *Rimāḥ*, in marg. of 'Ali Ḥarāzim, *Jawāhir al-Maᶜānî*, Cairo, 1927, vol. 1, p. 103, and vol. 2, pp. 231-244.

27 Ibrahima Marône, "Le Tidianisme au Sénégal," *Bulletin de l'IFAN*, vol. 32, n. 1, 1970, p. 210.

28 ᶜAlī Ḥarāzim, *Jawāhir al-Maᶜānī*, Cairo, 1927, vol. 1, pp. 114-116.

29 *Ibid.*

30 *Al-ḥājj* ᶜUmar Tall, *Rimaḥ*, vol.I, p. 120.

31 *Ibid.*, vol. 1, pp. 192-3.

32 *Ibid.*, vol. 1, p. 195.

33 Aboubakar Khalid Bâ, *Images de la lutte des musulmans en Afrique de l'ouest*, Nouakchott, 1980, p. 7.

34 Amar Samb, "L'Islam et l'histoire du Sénégal," in *Bulletin de l'IFAN*, vol. 33, no. 3, 1971, p. 38. This letter was written in response to a message from the Governor dated 13 August 1865.

35 The village of Thiénaba is about 15 km. east of Thiès.

36 These famous works have been standard in the corpus of Arab-Islamic education in Senegal for centuries. See the theses of Muhammad Ndiaye (1982) and Thierno Ka (1983), Université Cheikh Anta Diop, Dakar.

37 Paul Marty, *Etudes sur l'Islam au Sénégal*, 1917, vol. 1, p. 183-4. We would like to draw the attention of the reader to Paul Marty's antipathy to Islam and to his profound contempt for Blacks. We have used him as a source only when he can be corroborated by other sources. His positive portrayal of *Al-Ḥājj* Mālik Sy can be explained by what he called "the strong tendency of the written works of Al-Hajj Malick to be sympathetic to our [French colonial] cause," *ibid.*, vol. 1, p. 181.

38 *Al-Ḥājj* Mālik Sy, *Kifāyat al-Rāghibīn* , manuscript (see Bibliography), pp. 46, 53, 55, 74, 77, 81, 93, 96, and 136.

39 *Ibid.*, p. 55.

40 *Ibid.*, p. 33.

41 *Ibid.*, p. 219

42 Letter filed in "Surveillance de l'Islam," National Archives of Senegal, dossier 19G2.

43 See Muhammad Ndiaye, "L'Enseignement arabo-islamique au Sénégal," Dakar, 1982, p. 113. See also Khadim Mbacké, *Daaras et Droits de l'Enfant* , Dakar, 1994.

CHAPTER 5

44 Muhammad Bamba is better known by the name Khadīm al-Rasūl, "Servant of the Messenger," a sobriquet he chose for himself while in exile.

45 Mbacké lies 185 km East of Dakar. It was founded in the late 18th century by Muhammad Bamba's great grandfather, Maharam Mbacké .

46 Madiakhaté Kala was one of Senegal's most famous writers of poetry in Arabic. See Amar Samb, *Essai sur la littérature sénégalaise d'expression arabe*, IFAN, Dakar, 1972.

47 From the earliest days, the family of *Shaykh* Sīdī al-Mukhtār consistently maintained close relations with the Mbacké family.

The former transmitted to the latter the Qadirī *wird*, and this marked the beginning of cultural exchanges whose best aspects consist of numerous poems of remarkable literary value.

48 Paul Marty, *Etudes sur l'Islam au Sénégal*, vol. 1, p. 276.

49 These verses are from a poem by Ibrahima Diop Massar.

50 Paul Marty, *Etudes sur l'Islam au Sénégal*, vol. 1, p. 289.

51 *Ibid.*, vol. 1, p. 329 and 271.

52 *al-Muṣṭafā*, "The Selected," one of the names of the Prophet Muḥammad.

53 Muḥammad al-Amin Diop, *Irwā' al-Nadīm min 'Abd Hubb al-Khadîm*, manuscript (see Bibliography),p. 70 This author, who died in 1967 in Diourbel where he had been Imam of the Great Mosque, was a disciple of *Shaykh* Muḥammad Bamba . In the hagiography of hismaster cited here, he explained his master's vision of the Prophet in terms we have already described.

54 *Ibid.*, p. 23.

55 *Ibid.*, pp. 32-33.

56 *Ibid.*, p. 143.

57 *Ibid.*, pp. 30-31.

58 Paul Marty, *op. cit.*, vol. 1, p. 224.

59 *Minan al-Bāqī al-Qadīm fī Sīrat al-Shaykh al-Khadīm* has been published in French translation by Khadim Mbacké under the title "Les Bienfaits de l'Eternel ou la Biographie de Cheikh Ahmadou Bamba Mbacké". Dakar,1995.

60 Paul Marty, *op cit.*, vol. 1, p. 235.

61 We need to recognize here the courageous effort of *Shaykh* Abdoul Quddos Ibrahima Mbacké, one of Senegal's most educated and pious religious leaders, who never tires of explaining that birthright is contrary to Islam.

62 These deviations are privately recognized as such by the *'ulamā'* of the Mouride *tarīqa*. They maintain however that it is the responsibility of the brotherhood's leadership, and specifically of its Caliph-General, to combat the reprehensible practices. If he will not do it, why should they? The Caliph-General, for his part, sees no reason to condemn practices and behavior that his predecessors tolerated. Finally, the Mouride masses take refuge behind the tolerance and complacency of their spiritual leaders.

63 *Shaykh* Muhammad al-Bachir Mbacké, *Minan al-Bāqī al-Qadîm fī Sīrat al-Shaykh al-Khadīm*, manuscript (see Bibliography)vol. 1, p. 94.64 Paul Marty, *op cit.*, 1917, vol. 1, p. 248.

65 According to the *sharī'a*, wilful and conscious abandonment of any one of the five pillars of Islam is tantamount to apostasy.

Chapter 6

66 The Lebu (or Lebou), are a sub-group of the Wolof. They have been well studied by Assane Sylla, formerly a researcher at the Institut Fondamental d'Afrique Noire, Dakar.

67 Assane Sylla & Muhammad Saghir Gaye, "Les sermons de Seydina Mouhamadou Limâmou Lahi et de son fils Seydina Issa Rohou Lahi," in Bulletin de l'IFAN, vol. 38, n. 2, 1976, p. 24.

68 El-Hadji Malick Sarr, *La vie exemplaire de Limamoulaye*, Dakar, 1966, p. 29.

69 Mukhtar Lo, "La vie de Seydina Mouhamadou Limâmou Laye," translated from Arabic by Muhammad Saghir Gaye and Assane Sylla, in Bulletin de l'IFAN, vol. 34, n. 3, 1972, p. 57.

70 Mukhtar Lo, op cit., p. 16.

71 Mukhtar Lo, op cit., p. 30.

72 El-Hadji Malick Sarr, *La vie exemplaire de Limamoulaye*, 14-15.

73 Assane Sylla & Muhammad Saghir Gaye, "Les sermons de Seydina Mouhamadou Limâmou Lahi...," p. 11.

74 *Ibid.*, p. 7.

75 *Ibid.*, p. 9.

76 *Ibid.*, pp. 29-30.

77 Some Layèenes, like some Mourides, pratice an unlimited polygamy. This is a survival of pre-Islamic African traditions, and is contrary to Islamic law.

Chapter 7

78 These activities are designated by the term ziara, from the Arabic ziyāra, a pious "visit."

79 Moustapha Ndiaye, "Rapport entre Qâdirites et Tijânites au Fouta-Toro...," 1979.

80 Muhammad al-Fāḍil Mbacké (1886-1968) was the second Caliph of the Mourides (1945-1968). He was a fine Arabic scholar and a very generous man. ᶜAbd al-ᶜAzīz Sy (b. 1904) has been the second Caliph of Al-Ḥājj Mālik Sy's *zâwîya* since 1957. He is a most cultivated man, a superb writer, and is very modest and accessible.

81 The *ᶜĪd al-Fiṭr* marks the end of the month of Ramaḍān, the month of fasting and abstinence, and is determined by sighting the new moon.

82 *Shaykh* Aḥmad Mbacké was the eldest son of *Shaykh* Muḥammad Muṣṭafā Mbacké, first Caliph of the Mourides (1927-1945). He was a very cultivated man, and among the first *shaykhs* to send his children to French school.. He died in Touba in 1978.

83 *Shaykh* Muḥammad al-Murtaḍā Mbacké (b. 1924) is the youngest of *Shaykh* Muḥammad Bamba's sons. He is currently one of the *shaykhs* most committed to Islamic education.

84 The Tijānī *Shaykh* ᶜAbdallāh Niasse died in 1922.

85 Born 1909, d. 1990 see *ALA* IV, 350.

86 See Amar Samb, *Essai sur la contribution du Sénégal à la littérature d'expression arabe*, Dakar,: Mém.. de l'IFAN, no. 87, 1972

87 Both these compilations of poetry are preserved in the *Laboratoire d'Islamologie* of IFAN, in Dakar.

88 The Qurʾān was first printed in the Muslim world in Cairo in 1924.

89 The *Laboratoire d'Islamologie* of IFAN in Dakar has interesting examples of these in its collection.

90 Nocturnal ceremonies are held in all cities and towns on 12 Rabīᶜ al-Awwal (the third month of the *hijrī* calendar) to commemorate *al-Mawlid*, the birthday of the Prophet Muhammad (PBUH), but the Tijānī commemoration in Tivaouane is by far the largest of them all.

91 The *Magal* of Touba, the main event in the Mouride calendar , marks the departure of *Shaykh* Muḥammad Bamba for exile in Gabon. It has been held every year on the 18th of Ṣafar (the second month of the *hijrî* calendar) since the days of the second Caliph of the Mourides. It is habitually the largest Islamic gathering in Senegal and the number of participants keeps rising; 40, 000 were recorded in 1945, 250, 000 in 1947. Estimates today range in the area of one million.

92 Whereas the *Mawlid al-Nabī* is an official holiday, the *Magal* of Touba is not. Employees absent for that event must deduct the days from their annual vacation allowance.

93 Paul Marty, *op. cit.*, vol. 1, pp. 356-357.

94 *Ibid*, pp. 209-210.

95 Alphonse Gouilly, *L'Islam dans l'Afrique Occidentale Française*, Paris, 1952, p. 254.

96 Ibrahima Marone, "Le Tidjanisme au Sénégal", pp. 198-9.

97 The *Gamou* designates the celebration of the Birthday of the Prophet Muhammad (PBUH) on the night of 12 Rabīᶜ al-Awwal, and is a major event for the Tijânî *zâwîya* of Tivaouane (see above).

98 Ibrahima Marone, *op. cit.*, pp. 204-205.

99 A number of *shaykhs*, including Ibrahim Niasse and *Shaykh* Aḥmad Mbacké, continued to oppose this legislation, even after it passed into law. In an interview published in the Arabic journal *Sada as-Sénégal* on 1 January 1966, Ibrahim Niasse revealed that prior to independence a minister had contacted him through the intermediary of Lamine Gueye seeking his support for a campaign

to modernize Senegal's Islamic family law. He had categorically refused.

100 Some eye-witnesses have reported that during the 1988 presidential election, the Caliph-General asked his followers to physically prevent people from voting for the opppsition parties.

101 *Unité Africaine*, 30 January, 1978, p. 78, cited by Lucy Behrmann, *Muslim Brotherhoods and Politics in Senegal*, Cambridge [MA]:.Harvard University Press, 1970.

102 The *'ulamâ'* have used the term *mudārah* to describe the attitude to be taken in the face of a government one cannot or does not want to oppose publicly.

103 Consequences of the political activities of Muṣṭafā Sy, moral leader of the Mustarshidîn movement , can be related to deterioration of the relationship of his father, shaykh Tidiane Sy , and the President. Muṣṭafā Sy was arrested and imprisoned after a meeting of opposition parties on 16 February 1994, in which Muṣṭafā Sy was actively involved, and degenerated into a violent demonstration. He was released several months later, but not before his Mustarshidîn movement had been officially dissolved.

BIBLIOGRAPHY

The Holy Qur'ān: Basic text is in Arabic. Text with parallel English translation, by N. J. Dawood, London: Penguin Classics, 1994.

Encyclopédie de l'islam, nouvelle édition, Paris, 1913.*Encyclopaedia of Islam* (2nd edn.), 11 vols., Leiden: Brill, 1960-2002.

ALA IV: *Arabic Literature of Africa*, Vol. 4 " The Writings of Western Sudanic Africa", compiled by John Hunwick, Leiden: Brill, 2003.

AL-ASQALĀNĪ, Aḥmad b. ᶜAlī b. Ḥajar, *Sharḥ Ṣaḥīḥ of al-Bukhārī*, Ryadh, Dār al-Iftā', 1401/1989-90.

BEHRMAN, Lucy C., *Muslim Brotherhoods and Politics in Senegal*, Harvard University Press, Cambridge, Mass., 1970.

CRUISE O'BRIEN, Donal B., Th*e Mourides of Senegal*: the *political and economic organization of an Islamic brotherhood*,Oxford: Clarendon Press, 1971.

DIOP, Muḥammad al-Amīn, *Irwā' al-Nadīm min 'Abd Ḥubb al-Khadīm*, MS: Fonds Amar Samb, IFAN, Dakar.

DUPONT, Octave & COPOLANI, Xavier, *Les confréries religieuses*, Algiers: Adolphe Jordan, 1897.

GOUILLY, Alphonse, *L'Islam dans l'Afrique Occidentale Française*, Paris: Editions Larose, 1952.

ḤARĀZIM, ᶜAlī, *Jawāhir al-Maᶜānī fī fayḍ Sayyid Abī 'l-'Abbās Aḥmad al-Tijānī*, Cairo, 1927.

ḤAYDARA, Muḥammad Shams al-Dīn, *Qiṣṣat Dār al-Khayr* (The History of Dār al-Khayr), MS Fonds Amar Samb, K n° 15 e., IFAN, Dakar.

IBN AL-JAWZĪ, ᶜAbd al-Raḥmān, *Talbīs Iblīs*, Beirut: Dar al-Kutub al-ᶜIlmiyya.

IBN TAYMIYYA, Aḥmad, *al-Fatāwā*, Ryadh: Saudi Bureau of Education, 1401/1981.

ᶜIYAḌ, Aḥmad, *al-Taṣawwuf al-Islāmī*, Cairo: Anglo-Egyptian Library, 1970.

LO, Muḥammad Sakhir, *La vie de Limamoulaye*, trans. Assane Sylla & M .S. Gaye, MS: IFAN, Dakar.

MARONE, Ibrāhīma, "Le tidiansme au Sénégal," *Bulletin de l'IFAN,* série B, vol. 32, no. 1, 1970.

MARTY, Paul, *Etudes sur l'islam au Sénégal*,Paris: Leroux, 1917.

MBACKE, Ahmadou Bamba, *Masālik al-Jinān*, MS: Fonds Amar Samb, E n° 15a., IFAN, Dakar.

MBACKE, Bachir, *Minan al-Bāqī al-Qadīm fī sīrat al-Shaykh al-Khadīm*, MS: Fonds Amar Samb, E n° 6 a., IFAN, Dakar.

MBACKE, Khadim, *Daaras et Droits de l'Enfant*, Etudes islamiques, n° 3, IFAN, Dakar, 1994.

---, *Soufisme et Confréries Religieuses au Sénégal*, Etudes islamiques n° 4, IFAN, Dakar, 1995.

NDIAYE, Mamadou, *L'enseignement arab-islamique au Sénégal*, IRCICA, Organisation de la conférence islamique, Instanbul, 1985.

NDIAYE, Moustapha, "Rapport entre Qādirites et Tijānites au Fouta-Toro aux X1Xe et Xxe siècles à travers "Al-Ḥaqq al-Mubīn" de Cheikh Mūsā Kamara," *Bulletin de l'IFAN*, série B, vol. 41, n° 1, 1979.

SAMB, Amar, "L'Islam et l'histoire du Sénégal," *Bulletin de l'IFAN*, série B, vol. 33, no. 3, 1971.

---, *Essai sur la littérature sénégalaise d'expression arabe*, IFAN, Dakar, 1972.

SARR, El-hadj Mālik, *La vie exemplaire de Limamoulaye*, Dakar, 1966.

SUHRAWARDI, Abū Ḥafṣ ᶜUmar, *ᶜAwārif al-Maᶜārif*, printed in the margin of al-Ghazālī's *Iḥyā' ᶜUlūm al-Dīn*, Cairo, 1957.

SY, Al-Ḥājj Mālik, *Kifāyat Al-Rāghibīn*, MS: Fonds Amar Samb, C n° 15 a., IFAN, Dakar

SYLLA, Assane & GAYE, Muḥammad Saghir, "Les sermons de Seydina Mouhamadou Limāmou Lahi et de son fils Seydina Issa Rohou Lahi", *Bulletin de l'IFAN*, vol. 38, no. 2, 1976.

TALL, al-Ḥājj ᶜUmar, *Rimah ḥizb al-Raḥīm ᶜalā nuḥūr ḥizb al-rajīm*, printed in the margin of ᶜAlī Harazim's *Jawāhir al-maᶜānī.*

THIAW, Libasse (Limamoulaye), *Sermons* (manuscript), *Bulletin de l'IFAN*, série B, vol. 41, no. 1, 1979

ARABIC WRITINGS BY SENEGALESE SUFI AUTHORS

The following information, entirely on works already published, is mainly derived from *ALA* IV. That volume contains much more information in four chapters on Senegambia, including known mnuscript copies.

Abbreviations: Publ.= published; M.=*Maṭbaᶜa* (Press); n.d.= no date [given for publication].

ABŪ BAKR KHĀLID BA

Ṣuwar min Kifāḥ al-Muslimīn fī gharb Ifrīqiyya [Images of the Struggle of the Muslims in West Africa].
Publ. Nouakchott, 1980.

ABŪ BAKR SY, known as Serigne Mbaye Sy (d. 1957)

Ḥurūf Ṣalāt al-Fātiḥ
Acrostic on the words of the Tijāniyya prayer *Ṣalāt al-Fātiḥ.*

Publ. with intro. by ᶜAbd al-ᶜAzīz Sy Jamīl, and French trans., *Huruf: Composition à partir des lettres de la "Sallatul Fatahi" de Cheikhal Khalifa Seydi Ababacar Sy (RTA). Les ruisellements de la splendeur*, Dakar, n.d.

AHMADOU TALL (b. 1943)

1. *Dimensions de l'Islam selon le Coran et la Sounnah*
Publ. Dakar: Sicap Baobob, 1996.

2. *Niche des Secrets: recueil d'Arcanes Mystiques dans la Tradition Soufie*
A book of prayers with emphasis placed on their numerological significance. The principal language of the book is French, though the text of most of the prayers is given in Arabic.
Publ. 2nd edn., Dakar, 1995.

AHMAD BAMBA (d. 1927)

1. *Majmaᶜ al-nūrayn fī fawāʾid al-dārayn*
Dumont (1975), 12, says in consists of 59 sections, of which 19 are moral lessons
Publ. Casablanca: Dār al-kitāb, n.d.

2. *Miftaḥ al-naṣr fī duᶜāʾ laylat al-qadr*
Described as a collection of poems taken from the letters of "Shahr Ramaḍān".
Publ. Casablanca: Dār al-Kitāb, n.d.

3. *Minan al-Bāqī 'l-Qadīm fī muᶜjizāt 'l-rāqī 'l-makhdūm*
Composed in 1321/1903-4.
Publ. Casablanca: Dār al-Kitāb, n.d.

4. *Safīnat al-amānī al-munjiya li-qāriʾihā min sūʾ al-khātima wa-balāyā al-azmān*
Publ. Casablanca: Dār al-Kitāb, n.d

5. *al-Ṣindīd*
Publ. English translation by Moustapha M'backé, *Sindidi: the Most Perfect Prayer for Body and Soul*, New York: Khadimou Rassul Publications, 1987.

IBRAHIM NIASSE (d. 1975)

1. *Afḍal al-daᶜawāt li-bulūgh al-ghāyāt wa-nayl al-masarrāt*
Publ. Cairo: Dār al-Nahār, *c.* 1987.

2. *Baḥth fī thubūt ruʾyat al-hilāl*
On the question of sighting the new moon to mark the beginning of a month (especially Ramaḍān).
Publ. ed. Sh. al-Tijānī b. ᶜAlī Cissé, Casablanca: Maṭbaᶜat al-Najāt al-jadīda, 1996.

3. *al-Fayḍa al-jāriya fī maᶜānī al-Islam wa'l-ṭarīqa al-Tijāniyya*
Publ. Zaria: Gaskiya Corpn., n.d.

4. *Ḥadīqat al-anwār fī-mā iḥtawā ᶜalayhi qawāᶜid al-Islām min al-ḥikam wa'l-asrār*
Address given at the Emir's palace, Kano.
Publ. Kano:Northern Maktabat Press, n.d.

5. *al-Ḥujja al-bāligha fī kawn idhāᶜat al-Qurʾān sāʾigha*
Argument in favour of the recitation of the Qurʾān being broadcast, reflecting a controversy in Nigeria. The Emir of Zaria, Jaᶜfar b. Isḥāq, had argued against it .
Publ. Cairo, 1375/1956.
6. *Ifrīqiyyā li'l-Ifrīqiyyīn*
Response to an article by Archbishop Lefebvre of Dakar which appeared in *La France catholique* of 19 December 1959, attacking Islam and African nationalism. Analysis in Samb, *Essai sur la littérature sénégalaise d'expression arabe*, 223-6.

Publ. Lagos: Times Press, 15 Ramaḍān 1379/13 March 1960; trans Gane Samb Lo, *L'Afrique aux Africains*, with *Lumières sur la Tijâniyya*, and *Les Trois étales de la religion*, Saint-Louis: Association Sciences et Services dans l'Islam Eternel, 2001.

7. *Jāmi*ᶜ *jawāmi*ᶜ *al-dawāwīn*
A collection of collections of poems by *Sh*. Ibrāhīm, selected by Ibrāhīm Balarabe Jega from the "Great *Dīwān*" established by *Shaykh* ᶜAlī Cissé, apparently in 1374/1954.
Publ. Cairo: Muṣṭafā al-Bābī al-Ḥalabī, 1979.

8. *Kāshif al-ilbās* ᶜ*an fayḍat al-khatm Abī 'l-*ᶜ*Abbās*
Completed 18 Muḥarram 1350/5 June 1931, with a *dhayl* written on 8 Muḥarram 1351/14 May 1932. Written to promote the Tijāniyya, and to justify his claim to being the "master of spiritual emanation" (*ṣāḥib al-fayḍa*).
Publ. Casablanca, n.d.; Cairo: Muṣṭafā al-Bābī al-Ḥalabī, 1371/ 1952, 1380/1961.

9. *al-Khuṭba al-ḥamīda al-jāmi*ᶜ*a li'l-ḥikam al-mufīda*
Speech given at Kaduna in 1391/ 1971.
Publ. Zaria: Gaskiya Corpn., 1391/1971-2 (copy in NU/Hunwick, 62).

10. *Khuṭba jalīla*
On the occasion of the Prophet's birthday.
Publ. Lagos: Times Press, 1380/1960; Zaria: Gaskiya Corpn., n.d.

11. *Majmū*ᶜ *qaṣā'id al-mawlid al-nabawī*
Collection of seven poems celebrating the Prophet's birthday.
Publ. Kano: Oluṣeyi Printing Press, 1379/1959-60; Cairo: M. al-Mash'had al-Ḥusaynī, n.d.; Kano, n.d.

12. *Majmū*ᶜ *riḥalāt al-Shaykh Ibrāhīm*
Contains accounts of four journeys made by Ibrahim Niasse, partly in prose and partly in verse: two to the Ḥijāz; one into

southern Mauritania (called Gannār in Wolof), 1371/1951-2; and one to Kumase
Publ. by Mammad al-Maʾmūn b. Ibrāhīm Niasse, Cairo: Dār al-Nahār, n.d.

13. *Majmūᶜ thalātha majālis sunniyya maʾthūra ᶜan khulafāʾ murshid al-sālikīn wa-murabbī al-murīdīn al-quṭb al-rabbānī wa'l-ᶜārif al-ṣamadānī Sī. Aḥmad al-Tijānī*
Texts of speeches given in Kano (1372/1952-3), Katsina(1372/1952-3), and Kaolack (1373/ 1953-4).
Publ. Cairo: Muṣṭafā al-Bābī al-Ḥalabī, 1956.

14. *Nujūm al-hudā fī kawn nabiyyinā afḍal man daᶜā ilā Allāh wa-hadā*
Publ. Rabat: Imprimerie. Aminiyya, 1962. Translations: *Stars of the Good Way*, Paris: Imprimerie de Carthage, n.d.; *Astres de la bonne voie*, Paris: Imprimerie de Carthage, n.d.

15. *Risālat al-tawba*
Written 8 Jumādā II 1395/18 June 1975. Addressed to his Nigerian followers warning them against the false claims made by a Nigerian adversary of the Tijāniyya to the effect that Sh. Ibrāhīm's *Urjūzat al-tawba* amounted to a declaration of his having abandoned the Tijāniyya.
Publ. Beirut: M. Dār al-Kutub, 1975
Tanbīh al-adhkiyāʾ fī kawn al-shaykh al-Tijānī khātim al-awliyāʾ
Publ. Cairo: Muṣṭafā al-Bābī al-Ḥalabī, 1959.

16. *Trois oeuvres choisies, traduites et annotées de Cheikh Ibrâhîm Niass*:
i) *Lumières sur la Tijâniyya*
ii) *L'Afrique aux Africains*
iii) *Les trois étapes de la religion*
Publ. [Dakar]: L'Association Sciences et Services dans l'Islam éternel [ASSISE], 2001.

17. *Tuḥfat ahl al-ḥāḍira bi-mā yanfaᶜ al-ḥajj siyyamā bi'l-ṭājira*
Publ. ed. Sh. al-Tijānī b. ᶜAlī Cissé, Casablanca: M al-Najāt al-jadīda, 1996.

18. *Wajh al-taḥqīq fī kawn jāmiᶜ Madīna huwa 'l-ᶜatīq*
Publ. Ed. Sh. al-Tijānī b. ᶜAlī Cissé, Casablance: M al-Najāt al-jadīda, 1996.

IBRAHIM SAL (b. *c*. 1953)

A leading *muqaddam* of the Niassene Tijāniyya, who has toured Europe and the U.S.A. giving lectures.

1. *Maslak al-hudā li'l-suᶜadā' al-Tijāniyyīn*
Publ. Adapted French trans., *Le Guide du Parfait Tijânî aspirant à la perfection*, Beirut: Editions al-Bouraq, 1999.

2. *al-Risāla wa'l-wilāya wa-thamaratuhā al-fā'iḍa bi'l-fayḍa al-Tijāniyya*
Publ. Adapted French trans., *La Prophétie, la sainteté et leurs fruits*, Beirut: Editions al-Bouraq, 1999.

INDEX

NOTE: the titles *al-Ḥājj*, *Qāḍī*, and *Shaykh* are not considered in alphebetization; nor is al-, or b.= *ibn*.

ABOUT THE AUTHOR, EDITOR AND TRANSLATOR

KHADIM MBACKÉ is Director of Research in the Department of Language and Civilization, Institut Fondamental d'Afrique Noire–Cheikh Anta Diop University, Dakar. Senegalese by birth and education, he studied in Medina, Saudi Arabia, and at the Sorbonne in Paris before receiving his *doctorat d'état* from Cheikh Anta Diop University in 1991. His doctoral thesis dealt with Senegalese pilgrimage to Mecca from 1886 to 1986.

Since joining IFAN in 1979, Khadim Mbacké has translated numerous primary sources related to Islam in Senegal from Arabic to French, including two biographies of *shaykh* Muhammad Bamba Mbacké, a biography of *al-hajj* 'Umar Tall, a number of Muhammad Bamba's treatises, and a number of important political works by *shaykh* Musa Kamara and *shaykh* Mbacké Bousso. Khadim Mbacké has studied the full range of contemporary Islamic movements in Senegal—Sufi brotherhoods, Salafists, Wahhabis and modernists—and published books on the status of women in Islam, on inheritance and child rearing, and on primary education. He has contributed to the research of the Islamic Educational, Scientific and Cultural Organization, and of the Organization of the Islamic Conference, through the drafting of a Cultural Charter for the Muslim world and a number of studies on social issues and development.

Born in Turkey, ERIC ROSS is a Canadian citizen with degrees in Geography and in Islamic Studies (McGill University, Montreal). Since 1998 he has taught geography at Al Akhawayn University in Ifrane, Morocco. He has conducted research on Sufi brotherhoods and Muslim towns in Senegal and on cultural tourism and urban design in Morocco.

JOHN HUNWICK, professor emeritus of history and religion at Northwestern University, has focused his research and teaching on the social and intellectual history of Islamic Africa. His books include *Shari'a in Songhay*, *Arabic Literature of Africa II: The Writings of Central Sudanic Africa*, and *Timbuktu and the Songhay Empire*. He has edited *The African Diaspora in the Mediterranean Lands of Islam* (with Eve Troutt Powell) and *Religion and National Integration in Africa*, and is a founder-editor of *Sudanic Africa: a Journal of Historical Sources*. He is former director of the Fontes Historiae Africanae project of the International Academic Union, and has received awards from the National Endowment for the Humanities, the American Council of Learned Societies, and the Fulbright Commission. He is a fellow of the Ghana Academy of Arts and Sciences.

CPSIA information can be obtained
at www.ICGtesting.com
Printed in the USA
BVHW070222160521
607156BV00003B/448

9 781558 763425